Norman R. Rich (1921–2020)

Norman R. Rich (1921–2020)

An Appreciation

Geoffrey S. Stewart

Hamilton Books

Lanham • Boulder • New York • Toronto • London

Published by Hamilton Books
An imprint of The Rowman & Littlefield Publishing Group, Inc.
4501 Forbes Boulevard, Suite 200, Lanham, Maryland 20706
Hamilton Books Acquisitions Department (301) 459-3366

86-90 Paul Street, London EC2A 4NE, United Kingdom

British Library Cataloguing in Publication Information Available

Library of Congress Cataloging-in-Publication Data

Names: Stewart, Geoffrey S., author.
Title: Norman R. Rich (1921-2020) : an appreciation / Geoffrey S Stewart.
Description: Lanham : Hamilton Books, an imprint of Rowman & Littlefield, [2022] | Includes bibliographical references. | Summary: "This is a biography and remembrance of the late Norman R. Rich, who taught European history for many years at Brown University and Michigan State University, among other places. Norman Rich was an eminent historian, prolific writer, gifted teacher and warm friend to countless colleagues, students and neighbors"—Provided by publisher.
Identifiers: LCCN 2021033363 (print) | LCCN 2021033364 (ebook) | ISBN 9780761873129 (paperback) | ISBN 9780761873136 (epub)
Subjects: LCSH: Rich, Norman. | Historians—United States—Biography. | College teachers—United States—Biography. | History—Europe—Historiography. | Brown University—Faculty—Biography.
Classification: LCC D15.R53 S74 2022 (print) | LCC D15.R53 (ebook) | DDC 940.072/02 [B]—dc23
LC record available at https://lccn.loc.gov/2021033363
LC ebook record available at https://lccn.loc.gov/2021033364

♾™ The paper used in this publication meets the minimum requirements of American National Standard for Information Sciences Permanence of Paper for Printed Library Materials, ANSI/NISO Z39.48-1992.

To the Memory of Ning and Norman Rich

Contents

An Appreciation of Norman R. Rich (1921–2020) 1

Beginnings 3

Education 7

Spring and Summer of 1936 11

Oberlin and Berkeley 15

Conscientious Objector 19

Doctoral Dissertation 23

Whaddon Hall 27

Ning 31

Return to America 35

Michigan State 37

Providence 41

Lyme 45

Productive Years 49

Teaching 55

230 Arlington Avenue 61

Other Work 65

Retirement	67
Later Years	69
Passing On	73
Appendix: 1991 Holiday Letter	77
Bibliography of Major Works of Norman Rich	81
About the Author	83

An Appreciation of Norman R. Rich (1921–2020)

Norman Rich was born on April 19, 1921, and passed away on February 22, 2020, having lived a long and fulfilling life. Norman was known as an eminent historian and a prolific author, and he is remembered as a gifted teacher and valued mentor. In this, perhaps he was like many other college professors. Yet anyone who was lucky enough to have known Norman saw that he was remarkably different from most academics. He was unaffected, friendly, funny, free-thinking, and surprisingly knowledgeable about matters having no obvious connection to his main field of expertise. In the course of writing this appreciation of Norman, I came to conclude the driving force in Norman's character was his love of learning. Endlessly curious, he enjoyed exploration in all of its forms – whether by traveling, reading, researching, making new friends, or simply watching. Over a lifetime, Norman amassed an astonishing breadth of knowledge in history, geography, languages, music, art, architecture, literature and wine, to name only a few areas. In anyone else, this sheer breadth of knowledge would have been intimidating, but it was more than offset in Norman's case by his openness, modesty and sense of wonder.

I was a student of Norman's and through his kindness became one of his friends. My life was changed because of his example, advice and support. I came to Brown in September 1969 from a large public high school in Louisville, Kentucky. I was a fish out of water in the privileged and competitive world of an Ivy League school, short of money, confused and always a step behind. I missed the comfort of the Midwest, and to me the Northeast was forbidding, cold, indecipherable and closed. My grades were barely average. In fact, when I returned to Providence at the beginning of my junior year, I had resolved to transfer somewhere else at the end of the semester if things did not improve. Almost by chance, I took Norman's course that fall, and I was immediately captivated by his erudition, enthusiasm and accessibility. I began to understand history on a level that had escaped me before, and slowly I improved my writing and then my academic standing. With Norman's encouragement, I undertook an independent study project that ultimately turned into a combined honors/master's thesis. My senior year, Norman hired me to become the "grader" for his course, so I had the privilege of seeing him frequently. He and Ning welcomed me to dinner countless times, and there I learned from their example what a simple, well-lived life looked like. While Norman never told me exactly what he wrote in the way of a recommendation letter, I have no doubt that he was the reason I was admitted to law school.

I remained friends with Norman for the rest of his life, and in those subsequent years no week has gone by when I did not appreciate something that I learned from him. He taught me what careful research was; how to write clearly and concisely; how get past a problem's easy answers; and above all to simply relish the study of history. But he also imparted larger lessons. By Norman's example, I learned to trust my curiosity and contemplate my own biases; to suspect the popular and doubt the conventional; and above all to value independence of thought. Equally, it was Norman and Ning who showed me in their unassuming way a manner of life that was unpretentious, sophisticated, expansive and enormous fun.

Norman died two months short of what would have been his 99th birthday. I had for a long time planned to debrief him about his life. I finally got around to it in October 2019, when I spent several days with him and his daughter Ann at their house in Lyme, Connecticut. Norman had suffered a stroke a few years before, and this affected his mobility and stamina. His mind and memory, however, were as sharp as they ever had been. I have based this appreciation of Norman upon these interviews, as well as things I learned in our many years of friendship and from the indispensable memories and suggestions of Norman's three daughters.

Beginnings

Norman Robert Rich was born on April 19, 1921 in Cleveland, Ohio, the only child of Robert L. Rich and Margaret Henss Rich. Norman was of German extraction. Robert Rich's family had been German-speaking Pennsylvania "Dutch" (a corruption of "Deutsch"), and Robert's mother was an immigrant from Germany. Margaret Henss—who went by "Greta"—herself was born in Germany, but emigrated to Canada in the years before the outbreak of World War I.

Norman's origins were blue collar. His paternal grandfather was a house painter, and his father tried his hand as a tree surgeon and as an "expressman" delivering packages around the city of Cleveland. Robert Rich's education ended with high school, although he showed a passion for self-improvement. By his later years, he was widely read and well-spoken, and his energy for advancement was reflected in his career as well. Starting out as a clerk in a paint factory, he ended managing one. Robert had a keen interest in business and was an astute investor; when he died in 1971, he left Norman a substantial estate.

Greta Rich was a person of exceptional refinement and culture. She traveled widely across Europe as a young woman and spoke French and English fluently. She had a highly developed appreciation for classical music, art and literature, especially poetry. One of her great joys was to recite long passages of verse from memory. By all accounts, Greta was a forceful personality, perhaps because of the obstacles she was forced to overcome.

Greta was born around 1884 in the town of Barmen, Germany, in the conurbation known as Wuppertal. The region—Bergisches Land—was heavily industrialized, and her family was of modest means. At some point, Greta married a man named Hornich, but the union was short-lived. Greta left Germany for Canada in 1908, possibly to escape her unhappy marriage. There, she lived in Ottawa, attending to a woman of some wealth and status and teaching history and other subjects at the Ottawa Ladies College.

After Canada entered World War I in August 1914, resentment against Germans grew as the war entered its disastrous stalemate. The Ladies College was ordered to fire all Germans on its staff. Although it refused to do so, Greta left anyway and came to the United States in 1916. She settled in Cleveland, earning a living teaching at a private girls school in Shaker Heights. At the war's end, Greta began teaching French at the YMCA to returning servicemen. She successfully passed herself off as French until one day she slipped off a ladder and uttered a German epithet. Nonetheless, most people thought that Greta was indeed French, with one restaurateur confidently guessing from her accent that she was originally from Marseille.

Robert Rich met Greta while she was teaching at the YMCA. There was a substantial age difference—Greta was a dozen years older—and Greta had to arrange her divorce with the German authorities before she and Robert could marry. They wed in a civil ceremony in Cleveland in mid–1920 and moved into the simple frame house in the suburb of Willoughby where Norman grew up.

The Riches lived in a working-class neighborhood that was, if all-white, of broad economic and ethnic diversity. Census records from 1930 reveal that their immediate neighbors included a mechanical engineer, a practical nurse, a typesetter, a welder, a landscape gardener, a tube maker, a tailor, a pattern maker, an auditor, a tool maker, a bank guard, a surveyor and several traveling salesmen. The majority were second-generation Americans; their families had come from Italy, Czechoslovakia, Germany, Denmark and England. The houses were modest —the Riches paid monthly rent of $55 for theirs—but most families had enough money to buy a radio, a question the census enumerators asked that year.

Norman liked to reminisce about the family across the street, the Munis. The parents, Carmelo and Mary, were from Sicily. Carmelo worked as a paper hanger. There were five Muni children, including a son, Anthony, and four daughters, the youngest of whom was Norman's age. The Riches often invited the Muni daughters to a small country cottage they had purchased, giving the girls a respite from the crowded conditions at home. Norman often was sick as a child, and it was Mary Muni who looked after him while Greta was teaching. When Robert Rich died, the Munis held a wake for him, and Norman kept up with two of the Muni daughters for years.

It may have been this exposure to people of all social classes and backgrounds that led to one of Norman's most attractive traits: his lack of snobbery and his appreciation of—if not fascination with—other cultures and backgrounds. Although Norman would come to count among his friends Oxford Dons, German industrialists, newspaper publishers, and all manner of eminent intellectuals, he put little stock in titles or wealth and had no use for anyone who took themselves too seriously. He enjoyed the differences among people and invariably was drawn to those who had intellectual interests or artistic passions or who—above all—had a sense of humor and proportion about the world.

Education

Greta laid great stress on her son's education. When Norman was five, Greta resumed her teaching career at Cleveland's progressive Park School. She conditioned her employment on the school admitting Norman as a scholarship student. Norman thrived there. In 4th grade, he learned about ancient Egypt; in 5th about Rome and Greece; in 6th the Middle Ages. His 5th grade class performed Shakespeare's Julius Caesar, with Norman playing the part of Mark Antony. In 7th grade, they concentrated on the Renaissance, making a model of Florence from Plasticine and studying slides of paintings in the collection of the Cleveland Museum of Art. It was in these years that Norman, in his words, "fell in love with art."

Park School ended at 9th grade, and Greta determined that her son's progressive education should continue in Europe. She knew of a prestigious school in Germany—Odenwald—in Ober-Hambach run by a prominent educator named Paul Geheeb. Geheeb's circle included leading figures of the day such as French Nobel laureate Romaine Rolland and the rising Indian politician Jawaharlal Nehru. Geheeb was the classic pipe-smoking German intellectual – white beard, knickerbockers, white stockings. Fascinated by Eastern theology, he recited something from Indian religious texts at every meal.

Greta wrote Geheeb in 1935 to see if she might teach at Odenwald and enroll Norman there. However, under pressure from the Nazi regime, Geheeb had left Germany the year before, moving his school to Versoix, Switzerland. There, Odenwald was merged into a school called the Institute Monnier. Geheeb hired Greta to teach English at the Institute, "the school's curriculum was taught in French." However, the merger of Odenwald with the Institute Monnier had not gone smoothly, and Greta became annoyed at the disorganization of the place. She resolved to leave as soon as the first term was over.

Norman was 15 by then, already fluent in German and French, but still unaware of the gravity of the crisis overtaking Europe. Many of his classmates at the Institute Monnier were German Jews, whose families had sent them to Switzerland for their safety. The Jewish students were bitter at their treatment by "Aryans" and vented their frustrations upon non-Jews. Norman was among those bullied, never fully understanding that the anger he faced from his Jewish classmates was a reflection of the torment they and their families were enduring. In any event, Greta withdrew Norman at the beginning of the spring semester.

It may well have been that the circumstances of Greta's family distracted the Riches from the realities on the ground. In 1928, Norman had accompanied his mother on a visit to her family in Barmen. He remembered their poverty. They lived in a small, plain house, had an outdoor toilet and used old newspapers as toilet paper. Although no members of the Henss family had died during the First World War, they shared in post-war deprivation. Following their government's admonitions, the Henss's had invested their wealth, such as it was, in German war bonds, the government having promised that they would be provided for when the war ended. That, of course, did not happen; Greta's family lost everything, and soon the Great Depression fell upon them.

Greta and Norman again visited Barmen in 1935 on their way to Switzerland. By now things were looking up. The Nazi economic program had revived the German economy and—in Norman's words— Germany was once again a "going concern." Greta's family had neither embraced nor rejected the Nazi party, but members of the family joined Nazi organizations when it became a condition of employment. Hitler's oppression of Germany's Jews was unmistakable, but it seemed beside the point somehow, now that things were improving. This blindness, of course, is puzzling. Greta (and Norman) were fluent in German, so little should have escaped their notice. The Riches had many Jewish friends in Cleveland, the Park School had a substantial population of Jewish students and teachers, and the Institute Monnier was expressly a place of refuge for Jewish children.

Norman said that perhaps the greatest regret of his life was his failure to understand, then and in the next few years, the desperate plight of European Jews. He was far from alone in this regard and, at the time he and his mother went to Switzerland, he was barely more than a boy. However, the evidence of persecution was clear, especially in retrospect, and Norman blamed himself for not seeing it.

Spring and Summer of 1936

After withdrawing Norman from the Institute Monnier, Greta embarked upon a tour of Europe that was among the defining experiences of Norman's life. Norman referred to 1936 as "the incredible year," and any student of twentieth century history would have to agree with him.

They began in Italy. Greta and Norman first visited Florence, where they spent long days visiting the collections of the Uffizi and Bargello and wandering through the Duomo, long before crowds of tourists pretermitted such leisurely viewing. After having a "marvelous time" in Naples and Capri, they went to Rome and spent days reliving Roman history.

It was during this week that Norman was present at one of signal events in modern Italian history. On May 9, he and Greta followed the crowds down to the Piazza della Repubblica and onward to the Palazzo Venezia, where the fascist dictator Benito Mussolini delivered a speech from the second-floor balcony. Mussolini announced that Italy had triumphed in its one-sided war against Ethiopia and that Italian King Victor Emmanuel III was now emperor of Ethiopia. Mussolini proclaimed that:

> Italy finally has its empire. It is a fascist empire, an empire of peace, an empire of civilization and humanity.

The agitated crowd responded with shouts of "Vive il Duce" and "Vive el Rey".

The two then traveled to Spain. In Madrid, they were joined by Robert Rich, who was flush with Spanish currency, having bought his employer's Spanish accounts receivable at a discount. The family spent hours studying the Prado's collection, saw the opulent tombs, baroque architecture and extensive art collection at El Escorial, and even attended bull fights.

Spain was in turmoil. Train service was unreliable because many stationmasters were communists and had been ordered to disrupt communications. Even where trains did run, people pelted them with rocks. When Greta and Norman went to San Sebastian on the Basque seacoast, they found that the hotel had been invaded by anarchists who occupied its rooms and pilfered its food with impunity. As the Riches traveled around Spain, they saw trouble everywhere. There were frequent protest marches and political rallies and, upon returning from a side-trip to the Balearic Islands, they saw troops marching down to Barcelona. They left for France shortly before the military coup of July 18, which ignited the Spanish Civil War.

After passing through France, Greta and Norman returned to Germany. They again visited Greta's family in Barmen, whom Norman found had become more patriotic. Greta's uncle and cousins were employed by the Reich Labor Service, a public works program that was an arm of the Nazi regime. Her uncle, in fact, headed the Labor Service's local office, a post that required him to join the Nazi party. Nevertheless, Norman did not have the sense that war was coming; instead, there was optimism that Germany would once again enjoy prosperity.

After Barmen, they went to Berlin. By now, it was August. The 1936 Olympic Games were underway in Berlin, and their host—an old friend of Greta's—arranged tickets for Norman. Norman spent several days at the massive stadiums and venues Hitler had built. He thought that the arrangements had been "beautifully done" and saw no signs of the regime's malicious anti-Semitism. Norman was especially moved by the Germans' embrace of the American athlete Jesse Owens. Although later writers were prone to claim that the Germans distained Black athletes and that Owens' four gold medals were an affront to the racially-obsessed Nazi regime, the opposite was true. Owens was in fact something of a folk hero in Germany, and the audience chanted his name whenever he entered the arena. The success of Owens and other Black athletes, in fact, was a propaganda coup for Hitler: after all, who could possibly accuse the Nazis of racism when they were so welcoming of athletes from so many other countries and backgrounds?

Norman and Greta returned to Cleveland in late August. Greta began teaching, and Norman enrolled, at Western Reserve Academy, about 30 miles south of Cleveland. Norman stayed there only one year because his family could not afford even the reduced tuition the Academy charged. He spent his Senior year at Shaker Heights High School, living with family friends whose house fell within the school district. Norman thought Shaker Heights was an excellent school, the best of all the schools he had attended.

Oberlin and Berkeley

Norman entered Oberlin College as a scholarship student in 1938. His college experience was unremarkable. He joined a "house" (Oberlin's equivalent of a fraternity), played intramural sports, went on dates, and attended dances. Norman said that he found Oberlin academically uninspiring. Although his first interest was art history, Norman majored in history. His grades were so-so, and he did not bother to apply to Oberlin's honors program.

Norman said that his most interesting classes were ones given by two eminent German Jewish academic refugees. One was Georg Karo, an historian of the ancient world who had headed the German Archaeological Institute in Athens. Karo taught a course on the legacy of Greece and Rome, although he largely ignored Rome and instead spent his time lecturing about Greece. Karo also read the *Iliad* to his students in the original ancient Greek, believing that no translation could communicate the beauty and force of Homer's poetry. Another was Wolfgang Stechow, a Prussian who had survived imprisonment by the Russians in World War I and went on to become a leading authority on Northern European painting. Stechow also happened to be a concert pianist, and when Bela Bartok performed at Oberlin on December 3, 1941, Stechow played the accompaniment.

By then, most Americans had concluded that another world war was inevitable. When Greta learned in May 1939 that Germany had invaded Poland, and that the United Kingdom and France had thereby declared war on Germany, she burst into tears. "That awful man," she sobbed.

"He's done it. Leading these fine people. They're just going to lose again, and this time it will be even worse."

Soon after the Japanese attack on Pearl Harbor, Norman was required to register to be drafted into the military. He had already determined that his conscience would not allow him to serve in the military, however, and he inscribed on his draft registration card that he was "Registering as a Conscientious Objector." Norman's decision was not based on religious grounds. Although his father had come from a long line of Mennonites who abjured violence of any kind (indeed, one of Norman's aunts confiscated Norman's squirt gun when he was a child), Norman's opposition to war was not theological. Instead, he had learned enough of war from books, movies and other sources to believe that it was inherently inhuman. Norman said that he "just could not see the point of killing other people." Having already traveled extensively through Europe and seen the aftermath of the First World War, Norman's reaction to renewed global war was "My God! And for what?"

Norman graduated from Oberlin in 1942 knowing that he soon would be called up for military service and probably sent to a camp for conscientious objectors. The son of a family friend worked in a shipyard in Richmond, California, and he told Norman that California was a pleasant place to live and an easy place to get a temporary job. With his parents now living apart (his mother was teaching at a private girls' school in Dobbs Ferry, New York, and his father had found a job in Canton, Ohio), Norman saw no reason to stay in Cleveland. He moved to Berkeley, California, for the interlude, thinking that he might take some graduate courses in his spare time.

It was a life-changing decision. With so many young men waiting their turn to be called into military service, the University of California organized a special semester. As a public university, Berkeley's tuition was nominal, and its courses were open to anyone who bothered to register. Norman found that he much preferred a big university to a small college. And, in his words, "that was when my education really began."

Norman's most fortunate decision was to take a course taught by Raymond Sontag. Sontag's focus was European diplomatic history, but he also ranged into the economic, social and technological underpinnings of international politics. It took a while for Norman to warm to Sontag's approach because Oberlin's history program had, in Norman's view, over-emphasized social history. One day, he asked Sontag what other courses he ought to take, and Sontag recommended a course in medieval history taught by his "good friend" Ernst Kantorowicz. Kantorowicz hailed from a prominent Prussian Jewish family and, after fighting in the German army in the First World War, had embraced various right-wing causes. He began his academic career as an ardent German nationalist, writing a panegyric of Holy Roman Emperor Frederick II, whom he portrayed as the embodiment of German nationalism. He had become one of Germany's leading historians until he was driven from Germany in 1938 because of his ancestry.

Norman enrolled in Kantorowicz' course on medieval history. He "had never heard lectures like that before" and was soon enthralled by Kantorowicz' mastery of history, literature, music and art. Being a German, Kantorowicz was technically an enemy alien and thus under nightly curfew. But he welcomed visitors, and Norman soon joined other students who came by Kantorowicz' house in the evenings, often conversing in German. Exposure to an historian of such depth and cultivation opened new dimensions in Norman's thinking, and he made lasting friendships with others in Kantorowicz' circle.

Norman remained at Berkeley for three semesters, receiving his master's degree in 1943. While in the Bay Area, Norman also became involved in the nascent civil rights movement, which was being organized by the civil rights leader Bayard Rustin. Inspired by Mahatma Ghandi's strategy of passive resistance, groups of students held non-violent sit-ins at lunch counters, skating rinks and other places to protest racism. However, San Francisco was then, as now, a broad-minded place, and Norman and his fellow protesters were crestfallen when no one voiced any objection to their presence. Norman remembered years later that their biggest problem was finding minorities to join their protests.

Conscientious Objector

Norman was called up for military service in 1943 and invoked his status as a conscientious objector. Despite wartime patriotic fervor, he suffered few recriminations. At no time during his three years at the camp for conscientious objector did anyone from the local community distain Norman or his fellow COs as cowards or shirkers in the war effort. After the war, Norman wrote that he "encountered no prejudice or unpleasantness of any kind."

That having been said, the CO program itself was rooted in controversy. President Franklin Roosevelt opposed recognizing conscientious objection and relented only when representatives from the "peace churches" (Quakers, Mennonites and Brethren, to name three) pointed out how costly it would be to imprison thousands of COs and then argued that the COs might even be put to work on civilian projects. Roosevelt ultimately agreed, yet nonetheless refused to pay COs any form of compensation for their work (other than a $2.50 monthly allowance to buy personal items) or even appropriate money to pay for their maintenance. Instead, the government imposed a monthly fee of $30 upon the COs themselves. The peace churches usually paid this fee on behalf of their own members, but COs like Norman were on their own. Inevitably, it fell upon Norman's hard-pressed parents to pay the fee, but neither criticized Norman's choice. Notwithstanding the unfairness of charging the COs for the privilege of being confined to a labor camp, Norman reflected "[m]ost of us were profoundly grateful to our government for granting us this alternative, for we knew that under an authoritarian regime we would have been sent to a concentration camp or shot outright."

Norman was classified 4E, meaning that he refused to be associated with the military in any way. (There was another designation, 1-AO, for those who were prepared to perform medical or other non-combatant services.) He was sent to a former Civilian Conservation Corps camp in Coleville, California, in the high desert on the Nevada border. The COs there were housed in five large barracks and slept in rows of iron camp beds.

Coleville was operated by the U.S. Forest Service, and the CO's main job was to fight fires. The COs worked six days a week and, when there was no fire to fight, built stock trails and bridges, graded and repaired roads, strung barbed wire, felled trees for the camp sawmill, and handled such special projects as spreading arsenic-laced sawdust across the countryside to suppress grasshoppers. Although in later years COs were praised for their moral courage, Norman said he "never felt the least bit moral or courageous." The work was menial and unheroic, and Norman found out that a lot of it was done for the benefit of private ranching or timber interests. Norman and his friend Jim Clark spent months building a bridge over the East Carson River, later learning that it was for the benefit of a local rancher and used only on the rare occasions when the river was too high for his sheep to ford.

The camp had its share of eccentric characters, beginning with the inept managers from the Forest Service. Many of the COs were well-educated, and its population included professional actors and musicians, lawyers, writers, historians, economists and poets. There was a significant contingent of gay men, including some from England who emigrated to America in the 1930's to avoid the coming war, only to find themselves drafted by the United States. Men from various religious splinter groups also were interned at Coleville, including Jehovah's Witnesses and a contingent of Russian Molokans ("milk drinkers") who had come over years before to fulfill a religious prophecy. The Molokans—who, by now abjured milk in favor of stronger stuff—were large and boisterous men, given to frequenting the local brothels on their day off. There also was a sprinkling of Marxists, a small number of Jews, and a few Blacks. The saddest group were the "crazies," men suffering from acute mental illness who never should have been drafted in the first place and who were shuttled back and forth to a psychiatric clinic in San Francisco.

Norman was elected camp "education secretary." This meant he was responsible for obtaining books from neighboring libraries and finding movies to show. With money given to him by the Friends, Norman found that the Museum of Modern Art in New York had an impressive lending library of foreign films, although his fellow internees seldom understood or appreciated them. Norman also connived a way to build a swimming pool and tennis court for the camp. He persuaded one of the supervisors to let the men operating the camp's heavy equipment dig the hole for the pool and level the ground for the tennis court. They ran a pipe from a nearby spring to fill the pool and talked the highway department into letting them use left-over asphalt to surface the tennis court. Meanwhile, two of the English COs took over the task of cooking and were able to produce meals that approached edibility.

Life at Coleville was tedious and boring, and time weighed heavily. However, as Norman later wrote,

> I think most COs, for all our grousing, were very much aware of our good fortune to live in a country that allowed us to claim CO status, and that we were infinitely better off than the men who were defending the liberties to which we owed that status.

Norman and his fellow COs were kept in their camp long after the war ended. Perhaps to expedite his release, Norman volunteered for the United Nations Relief & Rehabilitation program to rebuild Europe. In July 1946, he took a bus to Savannah, Georgia, and joined the crew of a ship—the SS *DePauw Victory*—headed to the Dominican Republic to pick up a boatload of donkeys bound for Greece. Norman enjoyed his time at sea, but was appalled by the inhumane treatment given the animals. Many of them were in poor condition, and the ship's "awful" veterinarians were all too quick to put down sick animals. Dead and dying donkeys simply were thrown overboard as the vessel crossed the Atlantic, leaving a trail of carcasses in its wake.

After a stop in Gibraltar, the *DePauw Victory* sailed to Piraeus, close enough to Athens for Norman to see the spear of Athena in the distance. Given his love of classical art and history, Norman was awash in sentiment, but the ship's veteran crew was unmoved. "There are better whores in Savannah," they observed. At the last minute, the ship was diverted to the city of Patras—125 miles from Athens—to unload what remained of its cargo. The layover in Patras was brief, but Norman made friends with the British officer overseeing the occupation there and arranged for a seat on a supply vehicle making a routine trip to Athens. In what he considered an "incredible" moment, Norman found himself alone on the Acropolis, under a cloudless Greek sky, able to walk freely among the ruins of the Parthenon, the Erechtheum, and other archaeological treasures.

.

Doctoral Dissertation

Once home, Norman made his way back to Berkeley. His mentor Raymond Sontag was no longer there. In the course of the post-war occupation of Germany, Allied soldiers found 400 tons of records from the German Foreign Ministry that had been stored for safekeeping in salt mines throughout Germany. These would shed light on the origins and purposes of Nazi Germany's instigation of World War II, serve as evidence in the upcoming war crimes trials, and inform the inevitable post-war assignment of blame against Germany and finger-pointing among the Allies. The governments of the United Kingdom and the United States designated teams to review the war records with an eye towards translating and publishing the most significant ones. In 1946, the U.S. State Department appointed Sontag to head the American effort.

With Sontag gone, Norman was taken on by a scholar of Russian history, Robert Kerner. Kerner was of Czech extraction and particularly interested in Eastern Europe. He urged Norman to look into Nazi war crimes and aggression and suggested that he compare Nazi and Russian occupation policies.

Throughout his life, Norman was disturbed by the puzzle of Germany. It had been Europe's wealthiest, best educated, most cultured, and most scientifically advanced country. German universities were unsurpassed in their excellence; German scientists had, by far, won more Nobel prizes than scientists from anywhere else; German music and literature were admired globally; and German mathematicians, philosophers and thinkers had made one striking intellectual breakthrough after another. Yet, in the space of 30 years, Germany had been in—or caused—two catastrophic world wars, and everyday Germans had voted to elect a totalitarian regime that had systematically murdered millions of its own citizens. How had a country of such outstanding accomplishment descended into the enormity of Nazism and come so close to destroying European civilization itself?

One place to start was to look at the reasons Nazi Germany went to war in the first place, and Norman decided that his doctoral dissertation should focus upon Germany's motivations for World War II. He read Adolf Hitler's polemical book *Mein Kampf* and was taken aback at the openness of Hitler's plans for aggression. "My God. It's all there. Exactly what he was going to do." Hitler had written that the British empire could not last because its colonies were overseas and too difficult to control. Germany, however, would create an enduring empire of its own. Its colonies would not be overseas, but instead taken from the land next door, Russia, and populated with the German people. Once Hitler's objective was set, the rest of his agenda—the militarization of society, suppression of internal dissent, enslavement and ethnic cleansing of Jews and other "non-Aryans," the mythologization of the German past—were simply the means to this end or its byproducts. Norman's dissertation was titled "Nazi Expansion: Its Creed and Realpolitik." Decades later, he expanded upon the dissertation in his two-volume work *Hitler's War Aims*.

The edition of *Mein Kampf* Norman read may well have been a translation organized by the remarkable New York publisher Curtice Hitchcock. Hitchcock was among those concerned about the growing Nazi menace and, after British Prime Minister Neville Chamberlain's appeasement of Adolf Hitler in the Munich Crisis of 1938, Hitchcock determined that a complete, annotated translation of *Mein Kampf* should be published so Americans could see for themselves the dangers of Nazism. After acquiring U.S. rights to publish the book and fending off copyright infringers, Hitchcock assembled a committee of leading American historians and journalists (including Sidney Fay, John Gunther, and William Langer, among others) to edit, translate and annotate the book. (They were, in turn, overseen by a "sponsoring committee" comprised of famous figures of the day, including Pearl Buck, Albert Einstein, Edna St. Vincent Millay, and Norman Thomas.) Hitler's prose being essentially dreadful, the translation was edited to improve its readability, and the extensive annotations corrected *Mein*

Kampf 's flood of falsehoods. Hitchcock's publishing house made no profit from the book, instead contributing its net revenues (including royalties that otherwise would have gone to Hitler personally) to a charity assisting refugee children. Hitchcock himself, sadly, died an untimely death in 1946; had he lived, he would have been Norman's father-in-law.

Whaddon Hall

Berkeley awarded Norman his doctoral degree in June 1949. The same day, he received a phone call from the U.S. State Department asking if he would be interested in moving to England to become an editor of the captured German war records, the very effort Raymond Sontag had been heading. Norman accepted the offer on the spot and went to Washington to be introduced to the project. On September 24, 1949, he left New York on SS *Ile de France*, quite pleased that he had a first-class passage.

The German war records were originally placed in Berlin, but the British and Americans moved them to England after the Soviets block-aded the city in 1948. The editors were now working from Whaddon Hall, a former country estate 60 miles north of London. If the docu-ments' importance was unquestioned, their challenge was overwhelm-ing. The archive was immense in size – there were 300 tons of records from the period of 1920 to 1945 alone – it was both incomplete and overlapping; there was as yet no central index to the mountain of paper; and, of course, it was all written in German.

Norman worked at Whaddon Hall for five years, poring over the mass of Foreign Ministry materials, and selecting and translating the most important documents. He was one of three American editors at Whaddon, working with a slightly larger group at the State Department in Washington. There was a similar team of British editors, and also a group from France. Originally, the plan had been to publish 40 volumes of records embracing the entire interwar period, but the challenges of the project were so immense that in the end only 19 volumes—entitled *Documents on German Foreign Policy 1918-1945*—were printed, mostly concentrating on the narrower period from Hitler's accession to power in 1933 to America's entry into the war in 1941.

Among the members of the British team was a brilliant man named Max Henry Fisher, who went by the nickname "Fredy." Fisher was born in Berlin in 1922 and educated there until his Jewish family fled to Switzerland. At age twelve, and speaking not one word of English, Fredy was sent to school in England for his own safety. When war broke out in 1940, the local police arrested Fredy as an enemy alien; ultimately, he was put on a filthy and crowded ship to Australia, where he was interned in a camp in the Australian desert. When a change of policy finally permitted it, Fredy volunteered for the British army and was trained as a tank commander. He landed in Normandy on D Day + 1 and captained his tank all of the way to the Rhine. When the Allies occupied Berlin, Fredy was given the job of leading the British army into the city, since—having grown up there—Fredy was one of the few who knew his way around. After the war's end, Fredy attended Oxford, where he won a rare First in history. He then took a job with the research department of the British Foreign Office, and from there was assigned to join the team of editors at Whaddon Hall.

Fredy became, in Norman's words, "the best friend of his life." They collaborated closely in their work editing the captured documents, although Norman remembered having "terrible" fights with Fredy about which documents to include in the published war records. They had much in common besides their shared profession. They were the same age and still unattached. Both had German roots, and each had been confined to an internment camp during the war. They had a common love of good food and wine, although both were in short supply in post-war England. (Fredy's palate had been refined in the Australian internment camp, where one of his fellow inmates was the former head chef of the Savoy Hotel.) And they simply loved to travel. They bought a car together, a 1934 Wolseley Hornet Special, and "shared the joy of England."

They also made trips to the continent. One Easter, they bought plane tickets (for £10) and took a memorable trip to Paris. Norman had a somewhat exaggerated reputation for frugality, but it was nevertheless true that he simply hated to part with his money. Knowing this much about himself, Norman handed Fredy $100. "You can spend the money, since I never could spend it myself. Give us a good time." They went to the opera, saw the theater, traveled to Chartres and Versailles, and attended Mass at Notre Dame. On the flight back to England, Norman and Fredy were seated across the aisle from the well-known historian AJP Taylor, a Fellow of Magdalen College, Oxford. Taylor was a revisionist who had argued that Hitler was not the diabolical monster he was often made out to be, but instead an ordinary European politician with the unremarkable ambition to make his country as strong as possible. Other than his ruthless pursuit of power and his malicious anti-Semitism, Hitler had no overall agenda, and the onset of World War II was simply a tragic accident. Unfortunately for Taylor, the steady stream of German Foreign Office documents coming out of Whaddon Hall undermined these theories and even threatened to marginalize Taylor as an historian. After learning who Norman and Fredy were, Taylor bluntly said "I don't like you guys" and ignored them. (Years later, when James Joll, a German historian at New College, Oxford, again introduced Norman to Taylor, Taylor turned his back and walked away.)

The next year, Fredy met his future wife, Rosemary, who quickly became one of Norman's lifelong friends. Rosemary was from Australia, attending university in England. She met Fredy at a party Fredy had crashed in London; they found that they both were about to travel to Italy's Lake Como to see their families, met again there, and soon were together. Before long, Fredy asked Rosemary to join him on a trip to Wiltshire and Hampshire. But there was a marked difference in their ages and – to maintain appearances – Fredy asked Norman to serve as their chaperone. Norman recoiled at the idea, saying he had never chaperoned anyone before and had no idea what was expected of him. The trio nonetheless had a wonderful time. They toured Stonehenge, saw Salisbury cathedral, visited Winchester cathedral and its famous medieval Tournai marble baptismal font, and strolled the grounds of Winchester college. Norman particular enjoyed their lodgings in Winchester, an ancient inn called the Manor of God Begot, which Norman thought was very funny.

It was about this time that Fredy and Norman (each gave credit to the other) made perhaps the most important discovery of their careers. Allied troops had found German Foreign Office records reaching back to 1867, but the historians at Whaddon Hall confined their efforts to the period commencing in 1920. At some point, Fredy (or, perhaps, Norman) decided to look through the 100 tons of paper from the earlier period and found that they were sitting on an archival gold mine.

Among the mountain of diplomatic materials were the papers of the German diplomat Friedrich von Holstein, who had been a guiding force in German foreign policy in the last decades of the nineteenth century and the first years of the 20th. His papers included diplomatic correspondence, various memoranda, dossiers Holstein had quietly compiled on other officials in the German government, and even a secret diary. Holstein had been seen as a sinister character in German politics, and he was widely blamed for some of the German policy missteps that exacerbated international tensions in the years leading up to World War I. His papers, however, were more nuanced and cast new light upon the internal deliberations of the German government at a crucial time.

Fredy suggested that he and Norman should take on the task of editing Holstein's papers. This they did, spending years analyzing and translating the archives' content, with Fredy alone able to decipher the antiquated German handwriting script ("kurrantschrift") in some of the documents. The result of their labors was the *Holstein Papers*, published in four volumes between 1955 and 1963. The *Papers* were a uniquely valuable trove of primary material. Their appearance elucidated the policies of Otto von Bismarck and Kaiser Wilhelm II and Germany's complicated relationship with England. These were matters of contemporary relevance as well, since the question of Germany's guilt for causing World War I was itself now a factor in assessing blame for World War II.

Ning

Norman had a modest housing allowance from the State Department and, looking for something livelier than Whaddon Hall, decided to rent a place in London. One of his Quaker friends in the U.S. had suggested that Norman look up a prominent English Quaker who might have a room to rent. This was Lady Ethel Unwin, the widow of the famous architect and urban planner, Sir Raymond Unwin. In 1903, Sir Raymond and his partner Richard Barry Parker—who happened to be Lady Unwin's brother—had designed the planned community of Letchworth, which became influential in the planning of other model towns as far away as Stalingrad in Russia. He and Parker later laid out the larger Brentham and Hampton garden suburbs, all modeled on visionary principles of tranquility, open green spaces, and social and economic diversity. Unwin was knighted by King George V in 1932 and received the British Royal Gold Medal in Architecture in 1937. He also was a visiting professor at Columbia University, and it was in America that he died in June 1940.

Lady Unwin lived on Hampstead Heath at a place called Wyldes Farm, which she and Sir Raymond bought in 1906. Wyldes was among the oldest houses in England. It had an interesting history: Charles Dickens and his wife had lived there in 1837, and Dickens referenced the property in *The Old Curiosity Shop* and *Oliver Twist*. Norman rented a room at Wyldes, staying there on weekends. By now feeling very much at home in England, Norman also bought a dog—a golden

Labrador retriever he named Gigi—whom he took everywhere, including dinner parties.

Norman got on well with Lady Unwin, and she soon invited him to tea "to meet a young lady." This was Lady Unwin's American granddaughter Joan Hitchcock, who went by "Ning." Ning's mother, Peggy Hitchcock, had money in the U.K. that she could not expatriate to the United States because of Britain's postwar currency controls, and Peggy had suggested that Ning should go the England, take advantage of the money stranded there, and get to know her English relatives. Rooming with a friend from Bryn Mawr, Ning took a job in London as an editorial assistant with the *New York Herald Tribune*.

Ning's father was the already-mentioned American publisher Curtice Hitchcock, who had died—only 54—in 1946. Curtice was an accomplished and fascinating figure. He had been raised on a farm in Vermont and graduated from the University of Vermont in 1913. After a few years as a reporter for the *New York Times*, he worked in Washington as assistant secretary of the Council for National Defense and enlisted in the Army as a private as soon as war was declared.

For want of a better characterization, Curtice was a public intellectual. In the early 1920's he taught history and economics at the University of Chicago and, in collaboration with the famed economist (and, later, U.S. Senator) Paul Douglas, authored a much-admired study of labor relations entitled *The Worker in Modern Economic Society*. From there, he entered publishing. Curtice saw publishing as more than a business. A book was a "testing ground for ideas," he said. There is "always the exciting possibility of finding in book form, perhaps in a small and modest volume which only sells an edition of a thousand or so, a theory or a plan which may alter radically some vital human institution in the next generation." After a dozen years rising through the ranks at Macmillan, he and a partner started their own imprint—Reynal & Hitchcock—in 1933.

Although the firm lasted little more than a dozen years—and suffered acutely from the shortage of paper during World War Two—it compiled an impressive catalogue. In 1939, Curtice mounted the campaign to secure the publication of an accessible translation of *Mein Kampf* in hopes of warning the American public of the realities of Hitler's plans. Reynal & Hitchcock also published Lillian Smith's novel *Strange Fruit*, a groundbreaking best seller set in rural Georgia with a plot about lynchings and the taboo subject of interracial love. Other books ranged from works on political economy by the progressive businessman and politician Henry Wallace to the series of Mary Poppins books by the Australian-British writer Pamela Lyndon Travers. Yet another author in Reynal & Hitchcock's stable was the French author Antoine de Saint Exupery. The firm published the American editions of *Night Flight*, *Flight to Arras*, and *Wind, Sand and Stars*. After the fall of France in 1940, Saint Exupery fled to New York, where he began writing and illustrating his classic *The Little Prince* while staying in a spare room in the Hitchcock's apartment in Grammercy Park.

Curtice Hitchcock had been on a post-war mission to England when he met Peggy Unwin. They married in 1920, and Ning was born in 1927. Ning had grown up in an exceptionally stimulating environment, with roots on both side of the Atlantic and interesting people around her. Her mother Peggy was a committed Quaker, and Ning had been educated at the enlightened and progressive Friends Seminary in New York. For college, Ning went to Bryn Mawr, as a scholarship student after her father died, graduating magna cum laude.

Norman said that he was immediately captivated by Ning. Although he had a date that night, he spent the entire evening thinking of, and wishing he were with, Ning instead. He resolved to get to know her better, and so invited Ning to join him and another friend on a long-planned trip to Italy and Sicily.

Ning was no shrinking violet. It was said that as a young woman she could drink most men under the table; far from having a dainty appetite, Ning would finish her plate, and then eye those of her dining companions. Norman found Ning's energy and directness appealing, although Ning—who had no shortage of suitors—seems to have harbored doubts about Norman. Norman persisted, however, and family lore has it that Ning was finally won over by Norman's devotion to his dog Gigi: Ning concluded that anyone so kind and thoughtful to his dog would certainly be a good father, and maybe even a decent husband. In July 1952, Ning made a brief trip home to break off a relationship with one of her other admirers and to share her news with her mother and brother. After Ning returned in October, Norman paid the £1 license fee and married Ning in a civil ceremony at the Hampstead Register Office. To avoid inconveniencing others, they invited no one to the ceremony and had no reception or party. Norman remembered that this "succeeded in greatly offending everybody."

Ning moved into Norman's rooms at Whaddon Hall, but they continued to spend weekends at Wyldes Farm. Norman sold his share in the Wolseley Hornet to Fredy and bought a better car. They took frequent short trips, especially "to the sun" of the French Midi and the Spanish Costa Brava.

Norman was beginning to tire of Whaddon Hall. His friend Paul Sweet left his job heading the American team in England to return to other duties in the United States. (A few years later, Sweet would be elevated to head the overall State Department effort on the War Records.) Sweet's replacement was an unpleasant martinet who assigned Norman such menial tasks such as calculating the cost of groceries.

The first volume of the *Holstein Papers* was published in 1955, and Norman was offered a fellowship that year at Princeton's Woodrow Wilson School. He was flattered by the fellowship, which was essentially a means of helping him secure an academic job at Princeton or an equivalent place. In his own words, Norman was "riding high;" he was going from the center of the British academic world at Oxford to the center of the American academic world at Princeton.

Fredy, by contrast, was given no such break. He stayed at Whaddon Hall until 1957, vainly seeking an academic job in England. Given Fredy's brilliance and academic achievements, Norman saw no explanation for Fredy's exclusion from academia other than simple anti-Semitism. Fredy turned to journalism, starting out as a reporter for the *Financial Times*. There, he steadily rose to become its foreign editor, assistant home editor, deputy editor and, finally, editor-in-chief. Fredy transformed the paper from a respectable, staid business journal into the influential newspaper it is today. He expanded the *Financial Times'* international coverage, extended its reporting from the financial to the industrial sector, and added columns on business management. After Fredy retired from the *FT* in 1980, he went on to become a director of the merchant bank S.G. Warburg & Co. Fredy remained the best friend of Norman's life, and Norman was devastated when Fredy unexpectedly died, age 71, in 1993.

Return to America

Norman's time at Princeton was something of a disappointment. He missed the rituals of Oxford—the Senior Common Room, dining at the High Table, the collegiality of afternoon tea—and found the scholars at the Wilson School inaccessible. He also believed that he committed a career-derailing blunder. Also at Princeton then was another acolyte of Raymond Sontag, the historian Gordon Craig. Craig had recently published a highly praised study of the history of the Prussian General Staff. With his now-extensive knowledge of German diplomatic and military politics in the late nineteenth and early twentieth centuries, Norman found factual errors in Craig's book and ventured to bring them to Craig's attention. This antagonized Craig, and Norman believed it was one reason he was never taken in by the Princeton people.

However, Norman had come to the attention of yet another leading historian, the German-born Felix Gilbert. Gilbert, who was named after his great-grandfather Felix Mendelssohn, was among the group of scholars who had emigrated from Germany in the 1930s. Although Gilbert came from a well-to-do family, Germany's hyper-inflation had forced his family to interrupt his university education. He took a job in the German Foreign Ministry's historical section, where he helped edit diplomatic documents concerning the origins of the First World War. This, of course, paralleled Norman's work on the Holstein papers, and they became friends.

Gilbert was on the faculty of Bryn Mawr, and he offered Norman a one-year job teaching a course on the Protestant Reformation. Norman accepted the offer, only to realize that he had never taught anything before and knew almost nothing about the Reformation. Nevertheless, he put together a course, using as a basis his notes from Ernst Kantorowicz' lectures fifteen years earlier. One particular challenge was to get class discussions underway, but as the year progressed Norman found that he was an innately good teacher, probably because—as was said of Sontag—he genuinely liked his students.

Norman and Ning remembered their time at Bryn Mawr as a happy time. For Ning it was a warm and familiar place and, in her daughters' recollection, "everyone at Bryn Mawr just loved Ning." Ning worked as an Assistant Director of Public Relations in the college's communications office, and she and Norman enjoyed attending lectures on Oriental art, classical music, and other subjects. Norman appreciated the intellectually engaged, all-woman student body; he enjoyed his colleagues; and he liked the new and "very nice" Bryn Mawr campus. Bryn Mawr (unlike Princeton) allowed Norman and Ning to keep their dog on campus. Norman tethered Gigi outside the building during his lectures and the undergraduates fed Gigi and called her the "Poor Little Rich Dog."

.

Michigan State

Norman was a great success at Bryn Mawr, and the chairwoman of the history department, Helen Taft Manning (daughter of President William Taft) urged the college to offer Norman a permanent faculty position. By then, though, Norman had applied for academic jobs elsewhere. In late December 1956, Norman went to the annual meeting of the American Historical Association in St. Louis, where aspiring professors could look for open faculty positions.

The job market was difficult, and one of the few available opportunities was at Michigan State University. Predictably, there was a crush of applicants, but Norman was confident at the end of his interview that he had nabbed the job. His instincts were correct. Once that was out of the way, Norman immediately booked a trip to Greece for the coming summer. There, he and Ning used an unspoiled island near Athens as a headquarters while examining the area's ruins and archaeological sites. Ignoring admonitions against driving themselves around Greece, they rented a car and explored the Peloponnese, evoking in Norman memories of George Karo's lectures about the Greeks and the Myceneans. They took the ferry to Crete and marveled at the ancient ruins and the beauty of the Aegean Sea.

The return to the United States was a sudden dose of reality. They loaded their possessions onto a trailer and drove to East Lansing, and Ning learned that she was expecting. Housing was in short supply and they lived in part of a tar paper shack with a family that had "two kids and a screaming mother" until they found a suitable apartment.

Michigan State—its full name was Michigan State University of Agriculture and Applied Science—was a land grant college and less prestigious than the better-known University of Michigan. But Norman liked MSU's relaxed atmosphere and its lack of pretense, and he soon had administrative responsibilities. In 1958, he co-authored an influential paper on international cultural exchange programs proposing that Michigan State—and other universities around the world—should establish a system of fellowships modeled on the Fulbright grants for their own undergraduate and graduate students. Norman developed and taught the history department's general survey course on European history, as well as other courses and graduate seminars. Norman was given tenure in April 1962, and in 1966 he received the MSU Distinguished Faculty Award.

Norman and Ning enjoyed their years in East Lansing. It was in Lansing that the Riches' three daughters were born. The eldest, Margaret, arrived in 1957. The second, Ann, was born in 1959 and the third, Pamela, in 1961. Michigan was a pleasant place to raise a family, and Norman was a popular and appreciated member of MSU's faculty if, sometimes, a caricature of the absent-minded professor. His daughters told the story of a time when Ning was in the hospital about to give birth to Pam, leaving Norman in charge of Margaret and Ann. Norman had decided to turn the garage into a playroom and had begun repainting it. (Norman seemed to have a genetic attraction to painting things; was it because his grandfather had been a house painter and his father had managed a paint factory?) While their father was thus distracted, Margaret suggested to Ann that they should pretend to go shopping and hopped into the family car, which was perched atop a sloping driveway across the street from the Red Cedar River. The girls somehow shifted the transmission to neutral, and the car began rolling downhill. Fortunately, the car backed into a tree on its path to the river, staving off disaster. Norman had a difficult conversation with Ning when she returned home, and he never lived down the incident with his daughters.

Norman always considered Ning to be more talented of the pair. A case in point may have been Ning's graduate work. In the late 1950s, and despite the exhausting challenges of having babies to care for, Ning found time to enter Michigan State's graduate program. Beyond taking the required graduate courses and seminars, Ning wrote an enormous— 452 page—master's thesis on American policy in China between 1899 and 1912 and its usefulness as a test case for the economic interpretation of imperialism. She received her master's degree in 1962, and in 1965 became an instructor in MSU's Humanities Department.

During the 1962–1963 academic year, Norman took a sabbatical from MSU and, thanks to a Guggenheim Fellowship, became a Resident Fellow at St. Anthony's College, Oxford. Norman thoroughly enjoyed his time at Oxford. He and Ning rented a house, hired an au pair to look after Pamela, and sent Margaret and Anne to the local school. They took weekend trips around England and longer trips to continental Europe during school breaks. Norman enjoyed the habits of St. Anthony's High Table, drinks at the Master's Chambers after dinner and "all of the lovely snobberies of Oxford." But England lacked American luxuries of life. Norman remembered that he worked in an unheated room at St. Anthony's that had a Titian on one wall and a Velasquez on another "with his hands numb throughout the year."

Providence

Norman was now in his early forties and counted as one of the most promising historians of modern German history. As much as he enjoyed and appreciated Michigan State, he felt the need for a change and aspired to join the faculty of a better-known institution. In 1967, a position fell open at Brown University because of the tragic death in a car accident of Brown's rising star in German history, Klaus Epstein. One of the faculty members Norman had hired at Michigan State was now teaching at Brown, and he recommended Norman for the open position. Norman had mixed feelings about leaving Michigan State, but his regrets were tempered when he was able to arrange for his now-retired friend Paul Sweet to replace him.

Norman arrived at Brown in 1968, "a revolutionary year" as he put it. Protests against the war in Viet Nam roiled college campuses across the country, and Brown was no exception. At Brown there were walkouts by Black students; the intonation of the need for "relevance" in courses; the sudden, if half-reasoned, scrapping of traditional course distribution requirements in favor of a New Curriculum; and the adoption of a pass/no credit grading system for students who chose it.

Norman was quickly embraced by the student body. His year-long class on modern Europe diplomatic history—History 123 and 124—was among the most popular courses at Brown, and it attracted any number of students from other disciplines. He was friendly and accessible to his students and known for encouraging them to pursue historical tangents. Perhaps because of his own unusual upbringing, he went

41

out of his way to befriend students who did not fit the classic Ivy League mold. He welcomed, to his classes and to his home, students who were "commuters" (that is, local students who continued to live at home for financial reasons), foreign, or minorities. Norman was especially solicitous of the women students from Brown's coordinate college Pembroke. It was a known fact that it was harder to get into Pembroke than to Brown, and the "Brokers" (as they were known) generally were smarter than the "Brownies."

At the same time, Norman could be something of a puzzle. He did not advertise the fact that he had been a conscientious objector in World War II, but the fact leaked out anyway, giving Norman a certain currency during a time of anti-war ferment. Norman tolerated Brown's New Curriculum but had little patience for students who ignored foreign languages or failed to take advantage of the full spectrum of Brown's liberal arts offerings. He remained a serious academic; he saw no special cause for "relevance" in coursework, since almost by definition a rigorous liberal arts education would be relevant to the needs and challenges of anyone and was precious in its own right. Although he was encouraging to his students, he did not—like all too many of his colleagues at Brown and elsewhere in those years —indulge them or go out of his way to curry popularity. And, whatever his pacifist beliefs, Norman was no naïf about the grim realities of international politics. He distained war and armed conflict but had no illusions about its inevitability. In fact, his dedication to the field of diplomatic history arose from his conviction that the reasoned and realistic practice of international relations was the most promising way to prevent war in the first place. Norman's specialty—the European century between Napoleon and World War I—had been a period of enormous scientific, cultural and economic achievement, largely because of the success of diplomacy in limiting the number of internecine wars.

His also missed the collegiality of Michigan State. "At Michigan State, there was a party," Norman remembered. "At Brown, everyone worried about being overtaken." Still, he made good friends among his colleagues. He found Donald Rohr, a fellow professor of modern European history, "an extraordinary man," and he enjoyed the outspoken company of the mediaevalist Bryce Lyon. Years later, Norman and the American history professor Jack Thomas became great friends. Norman had immense respect for the prize-winning American historian Gordon Wood, and he enjoyed his discussions with Brown's professors of Renaissance history, Burr Litchfield and Tony Molho.

The move to Providence entailed many changes. The Riches bought a house at 230 Arlington Avenue, close enough to campus for Norman to commute by bicycle most days. Built in 1903, the house was a converted carriage house, big enough for a family of five, but snug enough to retain its wonderful charm. Gigi having passed away, they got a new dog—a Labrador retriever they named Pandora—who was, in Norman's words "all heart, no brain." Ning became a teaching assistant at Brown, a position she kept until she joined the faculty of Rhode Island College as an instructor in the history department.

Yet Providence was still something of a backwater, and the Riches were unpleasantly surprised by its narrow-mindedness. When Ning and Norman came to visit Brown in 1968, they were startled to learn that Ning could enter the Brown Faculty Club only through the women's entrance on the side of the building. The Riches were invited to join the exclusive Agawam Hunt Club but declined after learning that the club had rules against admitting Jews, Blacks and other minorities. Margaret, Ann and Pam were enrolled in the exclusive, all-girl Mary Wheeler School, only to find that its curriculum was significantly ahead of that of the public school they had attended in Michigan and that it took a long while to make friends with their reserved New England classmates.

There were other transitions at this time as well. In May 1969, Norman's mother Greta died at about age 85. Her life had not been an easy one, and in her later years she suffered from blindness and other afflictions. Greta has been variously described by those who knew her as "determined," "formidable," and "overpowering," and there is little question but that her forceful personality and great plans for her son were driving forces in Norman's life.

Norman at Easter, ca. 1923.

On horseback.

Young thespian.

Birthday, ca. 1929.

Norman and Greta, probably at Oberlin.

Norman's draft registration card. *Image from National Archives\Records Administration.*

(Left to right) Fredy Fisher, Donald Watt, Georges Bonnin, André Scherer, Jacques Grunewald, Paul Sweet, Ken Duke, and Norman Rich. Norman's dog, Gigi, is at the lower right.

Wyldes Farm. *Ceridwen / Old Wyldes / CC BY-SA 2.0.*

Ning, Gigi, and Norman.

Norman and Greta.

Norman at Michigan State.

Ning sailing on Long Island Sound.

Norman at the helm.

Ann and Norman Rich.

Lyme

One attraction of Providence was its proximity to Lyme, Connecticut, where Ning's family had long had a country house. Lyme quickly became a focal point of Norman's life and remained so for the next 50 years.

Like many New Yorkers, Ning's parents had aspired to have a place outside of the city where their family could spend weekends and summers. In 1925, Curtice and Peggy found an ideal spot at the high point of a meadow in Lyme. Lyme had been for some time a retreat for a wide range of interesting people. At the turn of the twentieth century, nearby Old Lyme (which, ironically, was younger than Lyme itself) became an artists' colony centered around a boarding house kept by a woman named Florence Griswold. Childe Hassam, Mary Wheeler, Henry Ward Ranger, Willard Metcalf, and the sisters Lydia and Breta Longacre were among the American impressionists who painted there. Because of its location near Yale, Brown and other universities, there was a fair sampling of academics, and any number of wealthy and prominent New Yorkers had homes there as well. (Peggy Hitchcock remembered, for example, the eminent jurists [and cousins] Learned and Augustus Hand fencing with fireplace pokers in her sitting room after one rowdy dinner party.)

The house Curtice and Peggy found was a classic, if ruined, New England saltbox on Grassy Hill Road. Even by the standards of Lyme it was old; there were indications that it may have been built as early as 1709. The structure was now in disrepair, and a local farmer was using it as a barn. For a modest price, the Hitchcocks bought the house and its adjacent acreage. It was, and remains, an exceptionally pastoral spot. There are a handful of equally picturesque houses nearby and a classic Congregationalist church down the road. The impressionist Guy Wiggins painted a landscape of the church around 1911, setting his easel directly in front of the house the Hitchcocks were to buy. Except for the fact that Grassy Hill Road is now paved, the scene is unchanged.

Curtice set to work repairing and renovating the structure. In this he was helped by his friends, one of whom was the prominent architect Richmond Harold Shreve. "R.H.," as he was called, helped Curtice reconstruct the crumbling fireplace in the center of the house, which included hoisting a massive stone lintel back atop its jambs. A few years later, Shreve and his partner William Lamb would achieve more lasting fame for their design and construction planning for the Empire State Building.

The Riches had a particularly strong attachment to Lyme. It was there in 1940 that Peggy's father, Sir Raymond Unwin, had died, and after Curtice Hitchcock suddenly passed away in 1946, Peggy struggled to hold onto the property. Ning and her brother John spent holidays and summers there as children, and Peggy now lived in Lyme year around. It was an especially welcoming house. The downstairs rooms of the original structure were warmed by the large fireplaces Curtice had rebuilt, a necessity in winter since the house was not insulated. There were comfortable chairs and sofas to relax in, and a dining room where eight people could be sandwiched as needed. There were antique side tables, cupboards, chairs and time-worn oriental rugs all over. Peggy stirred the fire with an old bayonet, affixed to a broomstick, that someone found on the property. The walls were hung with an eclectic collection of art, ranging from prints Peggy had collected during her years in Asia with the Unitarian Service Committee to Antoine de Saint Exupery's original artwork from *Le Petite Prince*. The bookshelves were crowded with first editions of Reynal & Hitchcock's books, and there were piles of magazines, book reviews, newspapers and books wherever a surface presented itself. The house was surrounded by lush meadows, and Peggy and Ning had created classic English gardens in beds beside the house, along an adjacent brook, and within the cellar hole where the colonial barn had stood centuries before.

Lyme was about an hour's drive from Providence, so the Riches often spent weekends there during the year as well as long stretches of the summer months. Lyme offered many diversions. It was surrounded by forests, and Norman and Ning enjoyed long walks through the woods. The nearby Eightmile River offered a swimming hole for relief on hot days. After his good friend Bob Webb taught him how to sail, Norman bought a small sailboat—Norman christened her the "Blueberry" (having rejected as imprudent the idea of calling her "Tenure")—which he moored nearby. When weather permitted, he and Ning liked to take visitors for an afternoon sail across Long Island Sound to Plum Island. They joined the Black Point Beach Club in Niantic and Mile Creek Beach Club in Old Lyme where they could swim and relax on summer days.

Lyme also was a convenient place for the Riches to meet Ning's younger brother John and his family. John and his wife Pamela lived in Toronto, Canada, where they were professors of urban planning. In 1960, Norman had guided John on a memorable six-week trip through England, France, Germany and Italy. John remembered that they drove a large black Opel Norman had borrowed from his German cousin Liesel and indulged Norman's passion for "venturing." In Germany, they happened upon a rural fair where they sat in a beer garden watching the locals (and, possibly, Norman himself) dancing the knee-slapping "schutplatt." This was, John recalled, Norman in his element. They traveled down and up both sides of the Italian peninsula, relying upon Norman's "doggerel Italian" to get them around. Norman especially liked Sicily, and he made sure that he and John saw much of it. They drove around the island, touring Taorima and Palermo, inspecting Monreale's cathedral, and visiting Sicily's many ancient sights. Since Norman, as John put it, "hated to part with money," the two stayed in various run-down pensiones, the cheaper the better. In Taormina, Norman suggested that they could save even more money by sleeping outside under the protection of beached fishing boats. All went well until dawn, when the police threw them off the beach, accusing them of trysting there. But they recovered from this misadventure and went on to travel across southern France and completed their memorable trip in Paris.

Grassy Hill Road was the center of a vibrant community that spanned generations. Frances and Helen Rosseau, longtime friends of Peggy Hitchcock, lived down the road in an historic house that had been the parsonage for the Congregational church next door. Ning had been a friend of their son Dick since childhood, and now Dick Rosseau and his wife Shirley were among Norman and Ning's best friends. (And, in turn, Dick and Shirley's children became close friends of

Margaret, Ann and Pam.) The Rosseaus were memorable for many reasons, not the least of which was that they kept a herd of sheep in a small field beside their house. Across the road from the Rosseau's was the modern house of Jim and Jane Griffin. The Griffins lived in New York but were fixtures on Grassy Hill Road on weekends and during summers. Jim was in the coffee business, work that had taken him to any number of unique places in South America and elsewhere. Jane was a doctor who spent her career caring for the poor, a fact made all the more telling because she was of ennobled British birth but, having been sent to the United States for safety during World War II, decided to remain here. The Griffins had a daughter and three sons, adding to the small mob of children found on Grassy Hill. Among Ning and Norman's closest friends were Bob and Lucky Webb. Norman and Lucky were prone to ferocious, if good-natured, arguments, which invariably ended with each being secretly persuaded by the other. As mentioned, Bob taught Norman how to sail, and the Riches were bereft when he died suddenly in 1971. The Webbs had four children, whom Margaret, Ann and Pamela Rich stay in touch with to this day.

Not too far away was Norman's fellow academic Sig Diamond and his much-adored wife Shirley. Sig was a professor of history at Columbia and had written extensively about economic history, political matters, and even an analysis of the life of Sigmund Freud. The Diamonds had two children, a daughter who became a doctor and a son who was my friend and classmate in law school. The community included dozens of other families as well—Harold and Barbara Goodwin, Paul and Penny Smith, Jeanette Behringer, and Jim McNair and Sy Silman, who was a professor at the Rhode Island School of Design and a former student of Josef Albers. Unquestionably, this list does not include any number of other dear friends of Ning and Norman, and their omission is entirely my fault.

Productive Years

Norman was a prolific writer and his years at Brown were among his most productive. He wrote a monograph on Europe in the late nineteenth century, produced yet another definitive two volume work, wrote numerous reviews and articles for academic journals, delivered lectures to both academic and non-academic audiences, and found time to write a topical and highly praised book cautioning against rash military adventures.

Norman's friend Felix Gilbert had been tasked by the publisher W. W. Norton & Company to develop a series of trade books on European history for use in college courses. He asked Norman to write a book on the period from 1850 to 1890. This came as Norman was about to embark upon a project to study Britain's pre–World War II Cliveden set, a group of upper-crust British socialites suspected of harboring pro-German sympathies. After accepting Gilbert's offer, Norman instead spent the year researching and writing his new book.

The result was *The Age of Nationalism and Reform*, which appeared in 1970, was updated in a second edition in 1976, and is still in use as college course material. Norman's decision to center the book on the rise of nationalism was telling. He considered much of the nationalistic impulse as inauthentic, often based on myth if not sheer confabulation. And nationalism could be destructive. It introduced centrifugal forces in Europe's multi-ethnic states, upsetting longstanding social and political balances and jeopardizing the future of minorities. Yet the ambitions of Napoleon and Bismarck's unification of Germany had unleashed this force, and its historical consequences were irreversible.

With this accomplished, Norman then returned to his long-delayed project of developing the themes he had analyzed in his doctoral dissertation about Hitler's objectives and methods in provoking a global war. He returned once again to the German war records, but was now focused on the tranche of documents from the wartime years themselves. His research required Norman to pore through records of the Nazi Holocaust, which left him profoundly disturbed and depressed. Among other things, he found in the files of documents from concentration camps the litany of peoples whom the Nazis had murdered, including many thousands of conscientious objectors like himself.

Although hundreds of books already had been written about Adolf Hitler and the Nazi regime, Hitler remained an enigma. Who was this man and what was it that he wanted to accomplish? Were his attacks on Jews, Poles, and others a core policy, or were they a calculated ploy to drum up political support from right-wing voters? Was Hitler really intent on starting a global war, or had he been bluffing? How had a man born into poverty in Austria somehow become Germany's dictator, subdued the country's powerful industrialists and respected military class, and intimidated even the Catholic Church into acquiescence? Was Hitler intent on dominance in western Europe, on vanquishing England and France for good, and avenging Germany's loss in World War I, or was he up to something else?

Norman approached the subject with his customary thoroughness and patience. After several years of research and writing, he produced a two-volume work, *Hitler's War Aims*, that appeared in 1973 and 1974. The first volume was subtitled *Ideology, The Nazi State, and the Course of Expansion* and the second *The Establishment of the New Order*.

The book landed in the middle of a spirited controversy on several fronts about the essential objectives of Nazi Germany. There were schools of thought that Hitler was simply another, unremarkable European politician; that he was a lucky opportunist; that he was a manipulative, micromanaging mastermind; or that he was mostly bluster and, but for the fact that the war spun out of control, would have been content with limited objectives. Few historians knew the original source material better than Norman, however, and his years of painstaking research confirmed to him that the truth was more direct. Hitler had a few overriding and overlapping objectives—centered on the creation of a land empire in central Europe and the dominance of a racially-pure populace within that empire—and Nazi policies crystalized around those seeds.

There was no greater authority on Adolf Hitler and his prosecution of World War II than the eminent Oxford historian Hugh Trevor-Roper. In an article published in the London *Sunday Times* in January 1974, Trevor-Roper gave the first volume of *Hitler's War Aims* a strong and positive review. This was an obvious slap at Trevor-Roper's longtime antagonist AJP Taylor, the very historian who had snubbed Norman and Fredy years before, who championed the "normal European politician" school of thought. After the second volume appeared, there were equally complimentary reviews in academic journals. German historian Klaus Hilderbrand favorably reviewed in *The Journal of Modern History* in September 1976. "Based on a detailed acquaintance with both the published and unpublished German sources and demonstrating a masterly command of the secondary literature," Hilderbrand wrote, "Rich's comprehensive study is bound to be definitive for a long time to come." Another notably punctilious critic, Donald E. Emerson, lauded the book in *The American Historical Review*, congratulating Norman on the exceptional thoroughness of his research. (Emerson observed with approval that Norman's first volume had 170 pages of text and 47 pages of endnotes.) He determined that Norman's thesis was correct: Hitler's war plans derived from his ravings in *Mein Kampf*, and the efforts of revisionist historians to ascribe other reasons for the war were almost beside the point. Emerson concluded that *Hitler's War Aims* convincingly "demonstrate[d] that only insistence on bringing the apocalypse of Mein Kampf to conquered Europe during the war explains the vast destruction of Jews and Slavs by governmental policy, which continued to the eve of defeat."

Controversy about Hitler continues to this day, but it was fundamentally altered by *Hitler's War Aims*. Norman's meticulous research changed the ground of debate about Nazi Germany, even if it led to yet new rounds of disagreement. Norman did all of this, of course, in his characteristically scholarly and modest way. Probably, he could have written the volumes for a popular audience, embellishing the more lurid details of the Nazi regime at the expense of historical detail. But those of us who knew Norman would have been surprised if he had done so. He was an extremely independent man, and he cared little for public accolades. For him, the measure of success was whether his work met his own high standards.

Norman's next major project—one that would occupy him for almost twenty years—was a treatise on diplomacy among the countries commonly known as the "great powers." However, he pursued any number of projects in the meantime. Norman was often asked to review recently published works by other historians, and his commentary frequently appeared in the *International History Review*, *Central European History* and other academic journals. Believing that history could be a useful lesson for contemporary decision-makers, Norman accepted invitations to lecture at the Naval War College in Newport, Rhode Island, and to contribute to the *Naval War College Review*. In March 1973, he delivered a lecture at the War College on "The Question of National Interest in Imperial German Foreign Policy," and he and Ning enjoyed their stays as guests there. (After meeting one particularly impressive Marine Corps General, Norman privately remarked that "the General—and his wife—were everything you'd expect a Marine to be.")

In the 1980s, Norman was alarmed by the saber-rattling of the Reagan Administration and, particularly, by its confrontational stance towards the Soviet Union. He saw troubling parallels between this belligerence and the diplomatic missteps that precipitated the unnecessary and counter-productive Crimean War of 1853–1856 between Britain, France, Austria and the Ottoman Turks on one side and czarist Russia on the other. The war dragged on until military losses on all sides and public discontent forced governments to negotiate a peace treaty that changed little. The war, however, ended the diplomatic arrangements known as the Concert of Europe that had kept the balance of power on the continent for 40 years.

In 1985, Norman published *Why the Crimean War? A Cautionary Tale*, a succinct and pointed treatment of the origins of the war. Norman viewed the Crimean War as a case of arrogance on the part of Britain and France, who could have negotiated a face-saving diplomatic compromise with Russia, but instead chose to make war upon Russia to elevate their own standing. That policy backfired: Turkey emerged bankrupt and weaker than ever; the war caused Russia to modernize and expand its military; Austria was isolated diplomatically and became easy prey for Prussia in their war in 1866; and the balance of power in Europe was never fully restored.

Norman wrote *Why the Crimean War?* for a public audience. He hoped to remind readers that aggressive foreign policies could backfire. Sometimes, they provoked wars that left matters even messier than before. The book hit its mark. It was favorably reviewed in both the popular and the academic press. A review in *The Journal of Modern History* concluded that "Rich believes that the outcome of the Crimean War contains some valuable lessons, the most important being that peace itself is the best means for maintaining stability and security in the international system." In the *American Historical Review*, historian Paul Schroeder wrote that "this book is important for historiography." "Although Rich does not claim novelty, the main points he makes … are entirely sound and ones on which, one would hope, this book will help establish a consensus." The eminent American diplomat and historian George Kennan praised the book as the "definitive work on the subject" and "diplomatic history of a wholly superior sort." "[I]t holds important lessons for the statesmen of our own age, if they care to consult them."

Of all the books he wrote, Norman reflected that he liked this one the best. He dedicated it to Peggy Hitchcock, who had died a few months before it was published.

Teaching

Norman genuinely enjoyed teaching and was exceptionally good at it. His signature course was the two-semester History 123 and 124 on European foreign relations from 1815 to 1945, the period defined by the end of the Napoleonic wars and the end of World War II. His classes were popular and well-attended, often by students who had not enrolled in the course, but simply enjoyed listening to Norman's lectures. Norman was a stickler for accuracy and detail. Thus, there were large maps of Europe on the walls of the lecture hall, which Norman used when explaining European geopolitics. He also believed in the essential importance of chronology as an historical tool. Norman often walked through the precise sequence of events in describing a particular historical moment, and his course syllabus recommended that students buy William Langer's 1,300-page *Encyclopedia of World History* for its exhaustive chronologies.

Norman was a compact man, and he always wore a well-tailored suit and a tie when he was teaching. (Ever parsimonious, he bought his suits for $15 at the annual Wheeler School clothing sale; fortuitously, another parent was exactly Norman's size.) When teaching, Norman tended to stroll around the front of the lecture hall, delivering his remarks from memory. He had two sets of eyeglasses—one for reading and the other for distance—and constantly switched them back and forth when he had to confirm a detail from his notes or identify a place on one of the wall maps. This confused everyone involved, since the two sets of glasses looked the same and one or the other was often lost in a coat pocket or pile of papers. Norman was completely absorbed in these lectures, adding illuminating details and never hesitating to stray into such subjects as the art, literature, or music—whether it was Wagnerian opera or Gilbert and Sullivan—when they helped to illustrate the tenor of the times. There was a radiator under one of the large windows where Norman liked to sit now and then, and occasionally he would leap up with an exclamation "That's hot!"

One of Norman's students, the historian Geoffrey Wawro, remembered these "wonderful, well-attended lecture courses on European foreign relations in which he gave voice to the people who actually mattered and the events that shaped history as we know it: Napoleon, Cavour, Bismarck, the Kaiser, the Moroccan Crises, war and peace." Norman's unassuming erudition was always on display. He could explain in detail the geography of central Europe and why a certain region was fought over, or ignored, or why a particular river kept popping up in the story. He understood the details of armaments and could explain with technical accuracy the twists and turns of the Anglo-German Naval Race in the years before World War I or why the weaponry of that war led to the stagnation of trench warfare. Norman lectured with such authority about military strategy and particular battles that no one would have suspected he was a committed pacifist. He had a wealth of anecdotes and insights about particular European politicians and diplomats, and he made even dry topics such as drawn-out peace negotiations, German hyper-inflation, and the complications of parliamentary coalitions interesting.

One thing that could never be overlooked was Norman's appreciation of irony and his sense of humor. He did not condescend to his historical figures as many of us do with our perfect hindsight, but he did enjoy making examples out of their follies. Thus, he would recite the fates of hapless Italian diplomats who failed to grab land when it was being carved up in one of Europe's periodic peace conferences; the pointlessness of the scramble for colonies in Africa in the 1880s; the buffoonery of Germany's Kaiser Wilhelm II, who insisted on wearing the uniform of a British admiral; or the sheer strangeness of European politics on the eve of World War I, when the King George V, Czar Nicholas II, and Kaiser Wilhelm II all happened to be cousins. No student forgot his couplet about Britain's construction of the battleship *Dreadnought*, which made all previous battleships (including Britain's own huge fleet) almost useless ("You have a brand-new battle fleet; it's five years old and its obsolete.") nor his characterization of Nazi Reichsmarschall Hermann Goering, who had an exceptionally high IQ, but was opioid-dependent and a pedophile. ("So, you see, he may have been a drug addict and a sex pervert, but he was certainly no fool.")

Norman never lost sight of the tragedies of history. There were wars that were avoidable, battles that never needed to be fought, people who were ever-oppressed, famines that were man made, countries that discarded democratic government for totalitarian regimes, and the unspeakable genocide of the European Jews. Despite his commitment to pacifism, Norman acknowledged that diplomacy alone could not pretermit these disasters. At a time when college campuses were upended by student strikes and mass demonstrations against the Viet Nam war, Norman did not subscribe to a simple, popular anti-war credo. War may be a last resort, but it would never disappear. Giving the example of the Poles in World War II, Norman had a memorable epigram: "People say that no one ever wins a war. That may be true, but countries sure as hell lose them."

It was a requirement of Norman's courses that each student write a well-researched, 30-page term paper. Norman liked to tell the self-deprecating story about the time one of his women students came to discuss a proposed term paper topic. Although an American citizen, she had grown up in Switzerland; this caught Norman's attention, and they had a pleasant conversation about various places in Europe. Her name was Kate Burton, and the subject she wished to write about was Sir Richard Burton, the famous British explorer, adventurer and linguist, whose command of Arabic was such that he successfully passed himself off as a Moslem and made the hajj to Mecca. Norman quickly agreed that this would be a good topic, then volunteered that this Richard Burton would be a much better choice than the famous—but completely disreputable—Welsh actor of the same name. Norman then had a chilling moment of realization. Wasn't the student named Burton? And wasn't it unusual for an American to come from Switzerland? After a moment's pause, Norman meekly asked whether the student's father might not just be the selfsame actor. Kate Burton confirmed that he was indeed, but tactfully added that she understood Norman's characterization. Still abashed, Norman invited her to his house for dinner, and the Riches soon considered her among their friends. Kate Burton went on to become a highly acclaimed actor.

Norman seemed to enjoy his undergraduate students as much as—if not more than—his graduate students. Their openness and energy appealed to him, and he encouraged them to pursue their interests. Sometimes, in the course of his lectures, he would mention a subject that had not been studied and suggest that a student should pursue it. In my own case, it was the odd fact that the Ottoman Turks had been rearmed in the 1870s with a massive number of powerful rifles manufactured in Providence. Norman's encouragement led me to discover, first, a hidden trove of documents in a Providence basement and, later, an overlooked episode of American economic history. Geoffrey Wawro wrote:

> The idea for the first book I ever wrote came to me in a class of Norman's. I saw a grainy photograph in a book he assigned of Austrian troops under attack by Prussian troops, and I asked him after the class if there was a book on that war, and he replied that there really wasn't. A decade later, *The Austro-Prussian War: Austria's War with Prussia and Italy in 1866* (Cambridge University Press, 1996) would be the result of that short colloquy.

In the course of his lectures, Norman would toss out ideas for research projects, ranging from the question why France's population remained steady for over a century (shouldn't someone research contraceptive practices?) or why the English political class—which professed neutrality during the American Civil War—had invested so heavily in Confederate "Cotton Bonds" that would pay off only if the South won.

Like other professors, Norman had set office hours when students could come by to discuss their papers. However, he made it clear that students were always welcome to drop in to see him—he quipped that research and writing was such tedious work that he always welcomed interruptions. Brown's History Department was housed in a musty Victorian house next to a gas station on Angell Street. Inside, the building was awkwardly divided into a rabbit warren of offices and storage rooms, echoing with the clatter of professors and secretaries alike pounding away on typewriters. Norman parked his bicycle in a back room—probably the house's kitchen originally—that doubled as the place where students were told to deposit their papers. If Norman's bike was in evidence, it meant that he was in his office at the top of the stairs. He kept the office in decent order, despite a daunting volume of books, papers, academic journals, and stacks of file boxes containing the thousands upon thousands of index cards memorializing his research. There were some pictures on the wall, although none seemed to relate specifically to anything Norman taught, and a visitor suspected that there might be a story behind each of them. Norman wrote at his desk, using a manual typewriter of startling antiquity, facing two uncomfortable wooden armchairs that had the unintended effect of hastening along the visit. Sometimes, the Riches' dog, Pandora, would be sleeping on the floor.

Norman was invariably hospitable. He often offered some anecdote about something he was working on or asked a student what they thought about a recent class. Norman's friendliness, though, was in contrast to his uncompromising professional rigor. The study of history should be an enjoyable and rewarding academic and intellectual exercise, but there was no place for shoddy research, intellectual shortcuts, or sloppy writing. And Norman eschewed conventional wisdom, politically correctness, or superficial analysis. What was important was for the student—or a professor, for that matter—to understand and confront the historical facts in an intellectually honest way, and to use the tools at their disposal to reach a sound historical judgment without preconceptions or regard for the popularity of their results. Norman did not particularly care where a paper, thesis or dissertation came out, provided the conclusion was based on sound research and serious thought.

Norman himself, however, had fixed ideas and strong opinions about the course of history. Facts were facts, and they had to be meticulously dug out, marshalled and respected. He was a traditional historian in his methods and interests and had no use for intellectual fads. More important than anything else was the history of politics—domestic or international—since the decisions made by those who ruled had the greatest historical consequences. Thus, whatever his intellectual curiosity might be about the quotidian, it was a waste of time to dwell upon "what the peasants ate." For similar reasons, he did not think that there should be historical specialties in women's history, Black history, or any form of ethnic studies. This seems almost antediluvian by today's standards, of course. It unquestionably reflected Norman's Eurocentrism, and it overlooked countless areas where historical methods subsequently made great contributions to our knowledge and understanding. But in his time, Norman was far from alone in his views that historians should focus their work upon those who governed. History had its lessons, and its purpose was to instruct. If two disastrous world wars had taught us anything, it was the importance of understanding international politics.

230 Arlington Avenue

Almost uniquely among the faculty at Brown, Norman and Ning extended invitations to undergraduates to come to their house for dinner parties. This was an unexpected honor; for all the talk of the benefits of attending a medium-sized college, instead of a large university, few students at Brown ever came to know faculty members well.

First-time guests approached the Riches' doorway with apprehension, but Norman and Ning quickly put nervous students at ease. Ning was an extraordinary hostess and an engaging conversationalist. A college professor herself, she could draw even the shyest undergraduate into conversation. She enjoyed talking about almost any subject, and her open friendliness quickly gave the evening a festive air. Norman, for his part, dispensed drinks and had countless funny stories to tell. In contrast to Ning's hearty laugh, Norman's was more like a cackle, and he enjoyed most of all telling stories about misadventures—his or others—often involving some disaster encountered while traveling or some absurdity of academic life.[1] Even more, he and Ning liked to talk about places they had visited, or planned to. Any student with travel plans quickly found themselves loaded with suggestions for towns, churches, museums, and ruins that they should see. And anyone who

---

1. Norman liked to tell the story about two of his colleagues in the History Department, one who constantly complained about his poor health and the other who never listened. The hypochondriac would catalogue his litany of physical complaints, while the other (usually flipping through his mail) would respond "Marvelous! That's so great! Congratulations!"

might have gone to a place the Riches had not yet visited would be pumped for information.

The Riches' house was itself a delight. One of Norman and Ning's most interesting talents was their ability to appreciate value in things others had overlooked. 230 Arlington Avenue was carpeted with beautiful oriental rugs that Ning had picked up in thrift shops in East Lansing when the mid-1960s craze for wall-to-wall carpeting deluded families into discarding their lovely antique carpets. The Riches' place settings were a mixed set of Elizabethan silver Norman and Ning had picked up in London from a shop that—in Norman's telling—was something out of Dickens, and atop the table were a pair of equally ancient silver candlesticks that Norman's wealthy English CO camp friend Dallas Doxford had given then as a wedding gift. The art on the walls was eclectic; in one corner was a lithograph signed by Georges Braque that Ning or Norman found in a shop when driving around the Continent, while elsewhere there were pictures whose artist and provenance were unknown. One wall of the living room consisted entirely of bookcases, holding everything from academic studies to murder mysteries to the Riches' large collection of classical music.

The dinners themselves were memorable. Ning was a superb cook; she excelled in making simple roasts or casseroles exceptionally delicious. Norman took special pride in serving good wine, but distained the expensive bottles found in the shops on Providence's East Side. Instead, he had found an Italian grocer who sold an excellent red table wine—I think it was called "Famiglia Cribari"—that came in one-gallon jugs with metal screw-on caps and was sold by the box. This was fortunate, since a tableful of undergraduates could quickly eat and drink a host—especially a college professor—out of house and home. And since Norman was careful to decant the wine into carafes, no one was the wiser.

The evenings passed all too quickly. Norman and Ning kept discussions alive and prompted even the most reticent student to join in. They found something for everyone to contribute and, in those rare instances where talk lapsed, they had interesting stories or observations of their own. One story was about the time they were in Sicily and, unable to find a hotel, were told to sleep in their car in the courtyard of the local Mafia Don's palace; the Don wouldn't mind and, besides, no one would rob them there. Another was about the time their friend Paul Sweet happened upon a particularly remote Romanesque church in southern France. He was delighted to find this obscure treasure, only to see from the visitors register that Norman and Ning had been there a few weeks before.

The Riches' interest in art and music was particularly appealing to students. Norman and Ning enjoyed remembering museums and churches they had visited and could talk about times years before when they had masterpieces all to themselves. Their genuine appreciation of art, and their comments on the pleasures of finding an especially beautiful fresco, mosaic or sculpture was inspiring to undergraduates who came from completely different backgrounds. Similarly, the Riches' appreciation of music could be inspiring. Whether Norman was describing the time Bela Bartok performed at Oberlin or the Berlin Philharmonic's visit to East Lansing, or Ning recounting chamber music she had heard in London, the Riches' casual, unpretentious refinement was an education in and of itself.

After dinner, the group usually would retire to the living room, in front of a warming fire in winter, continuing the evening with coffee or yet another glass of wine. The Riches' dog, Pandora, would wander in, and often their youngest daughter, Pam, would sidle into the room to eavesdrop. Invariably, the party was festive by now, and it was only with reluctance that the students took their leave after effusively thanking Ning and Norman for their kindness and hospitality. Faced with a mountain of pots, pans, dishes, glasses and silverware, the Riches' work was only beginning.

It would be difficult to fully express how much these evenings meant to the fortunate students invited to them. Living in dormitories, subsisting on cafeteria food, far from home, short of money, harried by deadlines, and anxious about their future, undergraduates found dinners at the Riches to be a high point of their entire college experience. Seeing how Norman and Ning lived opened a window onto another world. Their quiet erudition, enjoyment of life, and unfailing graciousness was a lesson each student took with them as they began the walk back to campus.

Other Work

Teaching and writing were not the Riches' sole occupation in those years. Ning had a lifelong interest in architecture and historical preservation. In the mid-1970s, she became active in the Providence Preservation Society, an organization formed in 1956 to prevent the demolition of historic houses and buildings in Providence's fashionable East Side. In her quiet and efficient way, Ning was instrumental in expanding the PPS' scope of work and making it a force in Providence's overall planning and neighborhood revitalization. In 1976 she began editing the PPS' quarterly newsletter but was soon elevated to the position of Coordinator of Neighborhood Projects. There, she was pivotal in taking the organization's work beyond the immediate environs of Brown and to all of Providence. This involved seeing people who had no use for run-down buildings and little appreciation for what the PPS did. Ning's expense reports from these years show that she had meetings almost every day, as often as not in the evenings, in all parts of town. Used to having Ning's company and excellent dinners, Norman grumbled about being left alone.

As a result of Ning's work, whole neighborhoods—the long-neglected blue-collar neighborhood known as Federal Hill was only one example—were saved from the wrecking ball. In addition, Ning supervised the research and preparation of a series of tour guide booklets covering particular Providence neighborhoods and helped establish a network of neighborhood preservation committees. By the time of her retirement in 1986, Ning was the Society's Assistant Director. At the function given in honor of Ning's retirement, Norman was surprised at the magnitude of what she had accomplished and abashed that he had been too self-absorbed in his own work to fully appreciate it.

Norman had projects as well, and one was the effort to recall the epically corrupt mayor of Providence, Vincent "Buddy" Cianci. Cianci had been a rising star in Rhode Island politics, becoming Providence's mayor in 1974 at the age of 33. As his mayoral administration unspooled, rumors circulated about his personal corruption, distain of the law, and haphazard style of governance. Cianci was re-elected in 1978 and 1982, amid growing concern over his dishonesty and thuggishness and the sense that Providence politics—never very clean—were getting even worse.

Things reached a breaking point in the early 1980s when Cianci fired Providence's Park Superintendent, Jim Diamond, for refusing to pad his payroll with Cianci flunkeys. Diamond happened to have been one of Norman's graduate students, and Norman joined the campaign to recall Cianci, knocking on doors and soliciting signatures outside of supermarkets. This had some personal risk. Cianci was protected by a coterie of corrupt cops, and proponents of recall endured late night visits to their houses by policemen claiming to be responding to unspecified citizens' complaints. It also introduced some awkwardness into the Riches' marriage, since Ning's preservation activities had brought her into close contact with the Mayor and she had even been awarded a medal by the City of Providence as thanks for her work.

The recall petition fell short, but soon thereafter Cianci resigned after pleading *no lo contendere* to a charge of torturing and assaulting (with the help of the Providence police) a man who was having an affair with his wife. (Cianci was again elected Providence's mayor in 1991, a position he held until his conviction in 2002 on federal racketeering charges.) In retrospect, Norman considered his work on the recall petition something of a waste of time. Interviewed by the *New York Times* about his efforts, he joked that Cianci's resilience showed "that you can't fight City Hall."

Retirement

Norman retired at the end of the academic year in June 1985. By then, he had tired of the bureaucracy at Brown and, in his view, the dilution of rigor in his profession. To Norman's disappointment, Brown discontinued History 123 and 124 after he retired.

Norman and Ning had long planned to spend their retirement years in Lyme. In 1999, they sold their house in Providence, surprised at high price the real estate agent suggested and astonished that someone actually agreed to pay it. Norman sold his extensive library to a book dealer, but soon regretted how much he missed it.

Norman continued to write. He had, for some time, been working on yet another ambitious project, an overall treatment of international relations in the modern era. This became another two-volume work, *Great Power Diplomacy*. The first volume, covering the period 1814–1914, was published in December 1991. Volume two, which brought the subject to the current period, appeared in 1992. Norman later updated the second volume, which appeared as a second edition in 2002. An ongoing challenge to the second volume was how he should deal with the breakup of the Soviet Union and its complicated aftermath, an instance of history in the making.

As usual, the books were well written. Norman's writing style was direct, unpretentious and efficient. Although accessible to the lay reader and intended for use in undergraduate and graduate courses, this work was again aimed at the serious historian. The major theme of the first volume was the instructive story of how the world's great powers had avoided a major war for a century, despite disruptions caused by the rise of new powers such as Germany, the United States and Japan and the decay of the Ottoman and Hapsburg empires. As before, the minor theme was a restrained didacticism. Norman wrote that his book "will not necessarily contribute to a solution of contemporary problems—these must be dealt with on their own terms and in the contemporary context—but some knowledge of how those problems developed and the experiences of the past should contribute to our ability to cope with them." The second volume dealt with the tragedy of the two world wars, the efforts by the international community to preserve peace, the Cold War, and the dissolution of the Communist bloc.

Great Power Diplomacy received favorable reviews. Stanford historian James J Sheehan praised the volumes as "[c]learly written, full of carefully chosen examples and sensible analysis." He wrote:

> Like many of the best students of international relations—beginning with Thucydides, the first and perhaps the greatest of them all—Norman Rich is a tragic realist. He recognizes that the inherent anarchy in the society of states makes struggles for power unavoidable; he offers us no utopian visions, no promises of perpetual peace. And yet he also knows that these struggles often have tragic results, always for the losers, but sometimes for the winners as well.

Sheehan concluded that *Great Power Diplomacy* was simply "the best single account of the diplomatic relations among the great powers from the Congress of Vienna to the breakup of the Soviet Union." Norman was pleased at the reception given *Great Power Diplomacy* but regretted it appeared at a time when colleges were de-emphasizing both European history and diplomatic history. He viewed it as a sad truth that those who decide the fates of nations rarely read history.

Later Years

The Riches settled into their retirement on Grassy Hill Road. By now, their daughters were grown and had moved away, Margaret and Pamela to the Bay Area and Ann to Chicago. Norman and Ning became active in local politics and causes. At Ning's urging, Norman became a Justice of the Peace, the main responsibility of which was to preside over impromptu marriages. Both Ning and Norman became active in local politics and made a point of attending fundraisers, speeches and similar events.

Ning continued her interest in land use and preservation. She joined Lyme's Planning and Zoning Commission and, to better understand the subject, enrolled in the University of Rhode Island's graduate program in Community Planning.[1] Her master's thesis was on the economic bases of historic preservation and gentrification of Providence's historic Armory District, and she received her second master's degree in 1991. Ever political, both Norman and Ning followed Democratic politics closely, and Ning became a member of the Lyme Democratic Town Committee. One of Ning's most enduring projects was her successful effort to preserve the pastoral landscape of Grassy Hill Road. She created the Grassy Hill Preserve at the top of Grassy Hill Road and with a small group of neighbors raised the money to preserve the land adjacent to the Grassy Hill Congregational Church from development.

---

1. Ning's mother Peggy had been one of the early directors of the Lyme Land Conservation Trust, and Ning joined the Board in 1993, ultimately becoming its Vice President. Ann Rich then served on the Board, the third generation of her family to do so.

Norman and Ning's life at Lyme had its customs and routines. They
rose early in the day and read or worked until noon. Lunch was a
leisurely meal usually consisting of salad, charcuterie, a few slices of
crusty bread, sliced vegetables, a glass or two of wine, and some fruit.
After a postprandial rest, Norman and Ning took an afternoon walk or,
in the summer, a trip to Black Point to read on the beach. Cocktail hour
was invariably a highlight of the day. Rosemary Fisher remembered her
visits to Grassy Hill Road. "Norman would make his dry martinis. He'd
sit back, cross his legs, have his wonderful smile, take a sip and everything would be all right."

Norman and Ning's love of travel was unabated. In 1989, Norman
went to Africa, where he visited Ning's brother John and his wife
Pamela who were teaching at the University of Malawi in Zomba. They
took a week-long side trip to Uganda and Zimbabwe, where Norman
particularly admired the ancient cave paintings in Matopo National
Park.[2] From there, Norman proceeded to South Africa, where he stayed
with an old family friend, Walter Hasselkus, who headed BMW's oper-
ations there. In 1991, Norman accepted an offer from the Brown Alumni Association to lecture on one of its voyages down the Danube and
then became a lecturer on the Semester at Sea program, a form of
abroad year where college students spent a semester aboard a ship
circling the globe. He and Ning enjoyed visiting places in Asia, Africa
and South America they had long desired to see. The next year, they
took a less enjoyable Cunard Danube cruise, but ended their trip by
attending the seventieth birthday party of Fredy Fisher. In 1995, Norman and Ning took a long-delayed trip to the Middle East, enjoying
Byzantine mosaics, retracing the steps of T.E. Lawrence, delighting in
the hidden Nabatean city of Petra, inspecting the now-destroyed ruins
of Palmyra in Syria, and wrapping up in Istanbul. Two years later, it
was Morocco and Tunisia, where they found the local people warm and
generous and a few of their fellow Americans embarrassingly crass. In
1999, Norman was once again the lecturer on a Brown Alumni Association Danube cruise, and in 2001 he and Ning went to Portugal. In
2003, Norman and Ning took an extended trip to Italy, once again

---

2.   However, Norman was dismissive of the eleventh century ruins of Great Zimbabwe, comparing them unfavorably to the cathedrals Europeans were building contempo-
raneously.

visiting Florence, Siena, Pisa, Lucca and Rome and reveling in the art and architecture of the Renaissance.[3]

2002 was the year of Ning's seventy-fifth birthday and Norman and Ning's 50th wedding anniversary. They held a party on Grassy Hill Road to celebrate. The event was held under the large maple tree that shaded the lawn on the south side of their house on Grassy Hill Road and attended by their family, old friends and Lyme neighbors. Pam, Pam's husband Dirk and their three daughters flew in from the Bay Area, and Ann came to Lyme from Chicago. The day was warm and bright, and it was an occasion to appreciate Ning's life and accomplishments and the contentment of Norman and Ning's long and happy marriage.

In these years, Norman also finished another pet project, a history of the much-maligned baroque era (1600–1750). He saw this as an opportunity to combine his interest in European politics with his abiding fascination with music and art. Unfortunately, the academic press already was under economic pressure; the publishing houses that Norman relied up in earlier years were cutting back on their offerings and laying off many of their most seasoned editors. In the end, Norman had to settle with writing a chapter for a collection of essays, *The Worlds of Johann Sebastian Bach*, which appeared in 2009.

Norman's contribution was a chapter on the historical background of the age, specifically concentrating on the politics of eighteenth century Germany. He argued that the much maligned, if now wobbly, Holy Roman Empire had been more forceful and effective than most historians had given it credit. On a cultural level, Norman maintained that art historians and musicologists had exaggerated the influence of French culture in German courts. The age was, he concluded, more multi-ethnic and cosmopolitan than commonly believed, with important contributions coming from the smaller German states, Poland and other places.

Norman's versatility and erudition would have been impressive in any case, but it is worth remembering that at the time he wrote this thoughtful and meticulously researched piece he was 88. He was, and remained, mentally acute and physically active. He and Ning still took their long daily walks; they enjoyed hearing from their daughters, granddaughters and in-laws, Joan and Marty Rosen; and they continued

---

3. Norman described these trips in delightful detail in the annual holiday card inserts he and Ning sent for years. I attach to this piece a sample of one, in this case his letter from 1991.

to see their Grassy Hill Road neighbors almost daily. Norman's interest in local, national and international politics was undiminished; he read newspapers, academic journals, histories, and novels continuously; he still drove his own car; and, most fundamentally, his curiosity about the world never left him.

Passing On

Around 2010, Ning began showing signs of decline. The initial symptoms were failures of memory, which then progressed to more serious conditions. Despite his own age—he was in his nineties by now—Norman at first insisted upon taking care of Ning himself. In 2015, Ning had the first of several falls and was moved to a nearby facility in Niantic. Despite Ning's dementia, she seemed happy there. Her daughter Ann remembered:

> While she was there, she received excellent care. They treated her well, giving her what became a favorite which was a thicker version of vanilla Ensure. To her, it tasted like a milkshake. She started losing a bunch of weight and her regular clothes didn't fit her any more. So they found her some "new to her clothes" including a pair of camouflage leggings and a purple top. Never in my life would I have ever imagined my mother in camouflage leggings. They would also blow dry her hair instead of doing a perm. My mother looked years younger than I had ever seen her. She looked fantastic. Despite not having much of a memory, she seemed happy where she was. I thinking she enjoyed having people take care of her for a change.

Ann also remembers taking Ning to Black Point in these last years. Ning was reluctant to take the trip, but soon put on her suit and entered the water. She had lost much weight and, in Ann's recollection, had an "amazing figure and looked like the actress Katherine Hepburn." Wading out into the water, Ning seemed to no longer have a care in the world; dementia had released her from her daily concerns and need to manage her life around Norman and her daughters. She saw the world anew, and now commented upon the loveliness of wildflowers or the beauty of the summer clouds.

Although Ning had more and more difficulty remembering people and events, Norman insisted upon visiting her every day. "It's what one does." Ning passed away on August 27, 2016. They had been together for sixty-five years, and she was irreplaceable in Norman's life. "It was the saddest thing in the world," he later said.

Norman himself was encountering the challenges of aging, although he was fortunate to have the devotion of his family to help him. In the summer of 2014, while Ann and Pamela were visiting Lyme, Norman suffered a stroke that incapacitated him from many daily activities. His daughters sent him to a local nursing home for rehabilitation, but he proved (in Ann's words) to be "a horrible patient." He was returned to Grassy Hill Road, where his daughter Margaret and brother-in-law John Hitchcock cared for him, rearranged the house, and engaged nursing assistance. In September 2014, Ann moved from Chicago to Lyme to take on these responsibilities.

Norman could be impossibly stubborn, and this became a challenge in his recovery from the stroke. He abhorred doctors and hospitals and resisted even the minor inconvenience of having nurses come to Grassy Hill Road. He strenuously opposed successive efforts by Margaret, John and Ann to arrange physical therapy, and relented only when Ann took on this job herself. Using a finely tuned mixture of promises and threats, Ann succeeded in overcoming Norman's reluctance.

> Eventually, after a while (and a few threats of if you don't do your exercises, you will not be able to stay in the house because it's not handicapped accessible), he got really good and disciplined about doing his rehab—to the point where he pretty much completely recovered from his TIA. It was pretty amazing!

Norman's recovery was such that, up until the last year of his life, he would take daily walks on Grassy Hill. Norman had remarkable mental acuity until the very end. In November 2019, I spent a few days with him to learn the details of his life that are recounted here. The effort of summoning up distant memories was challenging, especially since some of them triggered recollections of regret and loss, but Norman was able to recall a remarkable amount. Nor had he lost his powers of observation or analysis, his inquisitiveness, or his ability to place his life in perspective.

By early 2020 Norman was in declining health. In early February, his body began to fail him. Doctors were unable to diagnose any particular condition but recommended that he go to a nursing facility for short term care. Norman initially agreed, only to have immediate regrets. Ann and Pam's daughter Samara—who had flown out from California to help—persuaded Norman to move into hospice care, but it soon became clear that he wished to spend his last days at Grassy Hill Road. Ann wrote:

> Fortunately, Bill Webb was able to talk some sense into him and get him to voice what he wanted—to come home to die and say goodbye to his friends. Within a few days, Pam and Margaret flew out, we got him home, and arranged for hospice and 24-hour home care. The next week, Dad didn't eat anything, but he had a steady stream of visitors - long time Lyme friends. He came home on a Saturday and by the following Saturday, everyone who had expressed an interest in seeing him had paid their respects. There must have been 20–30 people who stopped by.

Norman died on Grassy Hill Road on the evening of February 22, without agony or pain. Norman's family and friends were in the next room having dinner and reminiscing about Norman when they had a sense that he had passed away. (In fact, his caregiver said that she saw his spirit come into the dining room from the living room and go into the kitchen.) Both Norman and Ning donated their bodies to science. As their friend and neighbor Rick Rosseau said, they were teachers both in life and in death.

Appendix

1991 Holiday Letter

230 Arlington Ave
Providence, R. I. 02906

Holiday, and all other greetings, come late this year, but the excuse is good. Ning and I have had an incredibly full year. In the spring, on the 25th anniversary of the Providence Preservation Society, Ning was honored as one of the 25 who had contributed most to the effectiveness of that society: reception at city hall, banquet, flattering speeches. She also finished her degree in Community Planning, and her diploma has just arrived to prove it, though it was not earned without a tiresome amount of bureaucratic hassle and pedantry. After a good deal more hassle, McGraw-Hill is finally bringing out the first volume of my diplomatic history, 1814–1914, which is supposed to reach me any day now, though I'll believe it when I see it.

Apart from that, there has been much travel. A Xmas card from a friend a year ago asked whether I would consider joining the faculty of a program called Semester at Sea for the fall semester of 1991. I would, and was duly appointed. But before that trip, Brown asked me to be the lecturer on a Danube cruise for two weeks in June and July—the first two choices for the job having fallen ill, and as I was being asked to do all the lectures, they would send Ning along for free. It was the kind of offer one couldn't refuse. So we were off to Istanbul in June, then over to the Black Sea to Ismael in what was still the Soviet Union but is now Moldavia, I believe. Transfer to a river boat, and up the Danube to Vienna with a stop at a long row of Bs: Bulgaria, Bucharest, Belgrade, Budapest, Bratislava. Fighting at Yukovar in Yugoslavia had already broken out, so we may have been the last cruise doing the length of the Danube this summer. A glorious trip, though Romania was drearily depressing and Bulgaria, though less dispiriting, was clearly in bad shape. Otherwise, the cities we visited seemed surprisingly prosperous, and Vienna positivity vulgar in its opulence—and prices.

Following Vienna, hectic weeks reading proof, preparing index, supervising map-making, and dealing with an incredibly inefficient publishing house, with my editor getting the sack the day before our departure for Semester at Sea, so that all plans for publicity and advance notice presumably went by the boards.

Ning and I had first heard of Semester at Sea when visiting a temple in Kyoto on our visit to Japan just after my retirement. There we met students who were taking part in the program, and we thought at the time that this was surely the perfect way to study a foreign culture. So we jumped at the chance of being part of the program ourselves. And it lived up to every expectation, though we were disappointed that the Gulf War changed the itinerary from Suez, Istanbul, Odessa, the Mediterranean, and Morocco, to Africa and South America.

We sailed from Vancouver, where we spent three days enjoying that city's spectacular setting, superb gardens, lakes, mountains, and the sea. Over the Pacific to Kobe, our arrival delayed by rough weather, which, as we are both good sailors, we thoroughly enjoyed. We were sorry, however, only to have three days for re-seeing Kyoto, Nara and Horyuji. In Japan everything works, but the dreary expanse of urbanization somewhat dampened delight in the oases of shrines, temples, and gardens, though the delight was nevertheless intense.

Communist thought it is, China too seemed to be working. We docked in Shanghai, a vibrant city, little sign of abject poverty, and a refurbished museum whose collection far surpassed the famous National Museum in Taiwan (or what was on display there when we saw it) and was the most impressive display of oriental art we had seen anywhere. We signed up for a trip to Beijing because our first visit there had been far too brief, and stayed at the guest house of Tsinghua Univ., China's MIT (or so they claim), with a lovely campus. In happy contrast to our first visit, perfect weather for the Imperial Palace, Temple of Heaven, and Great Wall. The city festooned with flowers to commemorate the anniversary of the Communist takeover. Here too things seemed to be in good shape, the markets full of food, no sign of beggars or other economic distress, but of course we only saw big cities ... and what we were shown.

We didn't have time to get the full flavor of the landscapes or anything else of Taiwan and Malaysia, but in both countries there seemed a fair degree of prosperity, abundant food in the markets. The National Museum in Taipei has wonderful things, but only a small part is on display at one time. In Malaysia we docked at Georgetown on Penang Island, an attractive colonial town, the island itself beautiful but being rapidly encrusted with high rise hotels along its beaches and in the hills. Given the great traditions of oriental art, it is sad to see how little is made of those traditions and how tawdry are the new shrines and temples, an incongruous assortment of Kitsch.

Madras was our port in India. a fortunate choice because just south of the city is a dazzling assortment of ancient temples—the province of Tamil Nadu. Here we hired a car and driver for what proved to be by far our most interesting visit, the glorious art offset by the extreme poverty and filth that we had expected, but the reality has to be experienced. As does the driving, which might be a thrill for sky divers and demolition derby enthusiasts, but went well beyond our desire for excitement. We survived, though we often wondered how, and now can recall with a certain calm the entire experience, a style of art neither of us had seen before and which we found fascinating, as we did what we were able to see and understand of religious practices—and human capacity for survival in conditions of poverty which went beyond even what we had anticipated.

In Kenya we docked in Mombasa, an old Portuguese-Arab port—the entire culture and population of the coast quite different from the inland areas with their agricultural economy, herdsmen, and game parks. Ning went on a one-day safari while I had desk duty, a great success—the safari, not the desk duty. The next day we flew up the coast to Lamu on the Somali border, the legendary home of Sinbad the Sailor. Lamu is an island, the only transport donkeys and dhows, those bird-like Arab sailing vessels which still dominate the waterways. Very few motor boats. How long will that last? The town itself white-washed adobe and brick, the roads only wide enough for donkeys to pass, the houses themselves low, the city still all of a piece with no high-rises, boutiques, or other signs of "modernization." A hippy haven a few years ago, so we were told, but they did no visible damage. Beyond the town, miles of beaches backed up by high dunes, the waters of the Indian Ocean radiant blue and perfect—if you like warm-water swimming.

In South Africa, apartheid was crumbling when I was there two years ago, and the process continues although we saw no dramatic signs of change apart from the shanty towns around the big cities which are growing at a perilous pace, swelled by rural migrants and refugees from Black Africa—Mozambique, Angola, Zimbabwe and points north. I must confess we had a marvelous time, thoroughly enjoyed the Dutch colonial towns, Capetown itself, the spectacular drive to the Cape and along the coast, and the excellent wines. One can only hope this lovely country survives the inevitable stresses of changes in leadership, because as of now it remains a going concern, in contrast to much of the rest of Africa.

And to what we saw of South America: Salvador (Bahai) in Brazil and Caracas in Venezuela. Abysmal poverty shanty towns, the old cities shabby and decaying, the new, high-rise and inhuman. Over population, environmental destruction, and corruption, which seem to be the dominant problems of the Third World . . . as they are of the other two.

The long periods at sea perhaps the best part of this entire incredible experience, suspended in time. Our final port, New Orleans, where the inefficiency in disembarkation was quite as great as anything experiences in India or Africa. The city itself, however, splendidly restored and attractive. We were sorry we had so little time there, but we arrived two days before Christmas and had decided in advance to avoid a hotel holiday.

That seems to cover everything worth telling, but does not mention the real purpose of this letter, which, besides sparing you the ordeal of handwriting, is intended to wish you all good health and good spirits for the coming year and many years to come!

Bibliography of Major Works of Norman Rich

The Holstein Papers: The Memoirs, Diaries, and Correspondence of Friedrich von Holstein, 1837–1909, M. H. Fisher & Norman Rich, editors. 4 vols. New York: Cambridge University Press, 1955–63.

Friedrich Von Holstein: Politics and Diplomacy in the Era of Bismarck and Wilhelm II. 2 vols. United Kingdom: Cambridge University Press, 1965.

The Age of Nationalism and Reform, 1850–1890. New York: Norton, 1970.

Hitler's War Aims. 2 vols. New York: Norton, 1973–74.

Why the Crimean War? A Cautionary Tale. Providence: Brown University, 1985.

Great Power Diplomacy. 2 vols. New York: McGraw-Hill, 1992–2003.

About the Author

Geoffrey S. Stewart lives in the Washington, D.C., area. He graduated from Brown University in 1973 with bachelor's and master's degrees in European history and received his law degree from Harvard Law School in 1976. He practiced law in New York and Washington, in private practice and government service, until his retirement in 2020. He is the coauthor of *The Anointed: New York's White Shoe Law Firms –How They Started, How They Grew and How They Ran the Country* (2021).